Raisins in the Squash:

a Recipe for Good Living and Financial Freedom

James R. Hollon, Jr.

First published January 2023

Ghostwritten by Sean Donovan www.Seandon.com

ISBN: 9798369710524

Imprint: Independently published

Printed in the United States of America

This book is dedicated to the betterment of lives, both individually and collectively in our society, as well as the preservation of the freedoms that are afforded to us, the citizens of the greatest nation in the world.

Contents

Foreword

My name is Dr. Gordon Klingenschmitt, and I'm a national TV host, former elected legislator, PhD Theology, former college faculty, and the former Navy Chaplain who dared to pray "in Jesus' name."

I'm writing to recommend the biography and testify to the high character of my dear friend Jim Hollon, who at the time of this writing is now 97 years old and a WWII veteran, one of the last living members of the greatest generation. He and his wife Shirley are philanthropists, business consultants, and "advanced thinkers" in the field of investment planning and kingdom strategy.

Jim is motivated by one powerful idea, that if charitable foundations governing over a trillion dollars of America's wealth would improve the efficiency of their investing, to reduce risk and improve returns through greater diversification, much new wealth would be created to be given away to actually serve many more among the poor.

It's a profound idea, and it takes patience to understand, but just imagine if what Jim is saying were true: that all charity leaders could implement the Hollon strategy to grow their nest egg faster, while reducing risks and fees, and simultaneously giving away more wealth to the poor than ever before, and growing their influence exponentially forever?

Jim's vision would change the world for good for the next hundred or thousand years, leaving a legacy to humanity that would out last his own life, and yours and mine, and change the world.

Jim has not only written about this, he has implemented it, and given his own wealth to make it happen within our small but growing charity. Yet his real legacy could also be given to you, now in the pages of this book, if you have Jim's patience, resolve, and advanced thinking that I've grown to love and respect.

I pray you enjoy this biography of my friend, Jim Hollon.

Chaplain Gordon Klingenschmitt, PhD

Pray In Jesus Name Ministries

Meeting Mr. Hollon
Ghostwriter's Preface

I came to know James Hollon by way of referral from someone who I admire and respect. From the moment Mr. Hollon called me, I knew I liked him, although I had no precise idea why. Little did I know how much we have in common, and how profound the relationship was destined to be. He shared with me his first book, *The Deferred Compensation Plan: How to Use Innovative Corporate Strategies to Maximize Your Benefits & Give Your Corporation a Tax Break,* by promptly overnighting it to me. I read it in one sitting and found the information to be very interesting and still relevant, 26 years after its publication. We talked again by phone about his ideas for a second book, and he sent me his notes and thoughts for this manuscript. Although we pretty much struck a deal on this book by phone and email, he made it clear to me that he "needed to look a man in the eye and shake his hand before doing business with him." I respect that, and I was happy to make the 7-hour drive to Satsuma, Alabama to meet him in person.

I received thorough directions to his house and specific instructions on where to park in his driveway, which was an immediate clue as to what a detail-oriented planner this man is. I had no idea what to expect, but when I arrived, I was pleasantly surprised to find that his two vehicles were of the same brand and color as mine. Right away, I knew we had something in common. It was also a great icebreaker to get us started; however, I would quickly discover that there's rarely a shortage of conversation with Mr. Hollon. When a man twice my age, with his experiences and successes, speaks, I listen with both ears.

It was a mid-August day in Southern Alabama, and the temperature display on my dashboard read 97 degrees. The humidity was probably 97%, the heat index was well over 100, and not a hint of a breeze stirred across the well-manicured lawn. An ordinary person would seek refuge and reprieve from the brutality of the heat in the comfort of their air-conditioned home. Spoiler alert – I'll just tell you now, so you can learn right up front like I did, Mr. Hollon is no ordinary man.

There he sat on his open-air back porch, wearing a long-sleeved, button-down shirt, long, black dress pants, and his head was topped off with a fedora hat. He reminded me of my own grandfather at first glance. Despite the oppressive heat, he was dressed appropriately for a business meeting. When I pulled up, he stood up and approached me with a smile and an extended hand. He walked confidently and proudly. Not only was his posture good, but his handshake was unexpectedly firm for a man his age; a trait I would learn is quite important to him.

I couldn't wait to get back into the a/c; however, I was immediately intrigued by his backyard. A large, deep-water creek adjoined his property, and a boat house and a treehouse-looking screened-in gazebo on stilts melded the water with the land. A sign was prominently displayed above the door to the gazebo; it read, *The Extras*. When I inquired about the meaning of the sign, he said, "God gave us two things: necessities and extras. That's one of the extras." He smiled as he pointed down the long, elevated, wooden walkway that led to the gazebo. "I'll give you a tour, but first let me show you some necessities."

I was eager to see the inside of the gazebo, but I was even more excited to see the terraced garden that inhabited the better part of the sloping backyard.

"You've got to eat, so this is one of my necessities," he says with pride as he points to the garden and proceeds to show me his watering setup and planting system. He took great pleasure and pride in showing off the actual fruits of his labor and explaining each and every plant. As a gardener myself, it was quite easy to recognize the thought, planning, attention to detail, and back-breaking labor that went into maintaining this victory garden. To this man, a well-kept garden is a more impressive display of success than the material possessions that most people consider requisites of success.

"You reap what you sow," he proclaimed. "Investing and managing money is a lot like gardening. Plant nothing, and you get nothing later. My plants started out as seeds," he said as he pointed into his germination greenhouse. "Planting seeds, right from the start, promotes hope for tomorrow. Think of seeds as your investment capital; plant them in fertile soil and they'll grow. But if you don't tend to your garden, the plants get overrun with weeds, kind of like your investments do with fees, etc. Not enough water, and the plants shrivel up and die. To prepare for droughts, you've got to move funds and diversify, and stay put for the long run, or your money will wither away. Don't harvest on time, the fruit rots on the vine; timing is important in the financial world, too."

The combination of my observations and the points he verbalized made me realize that how you do anything is typically how you do everything. This man has tended to his family, his finances, his business, and his clients in the same fashion that he tends to his garden.

Even with my short-sleeved, paper-thin, button-down shirt on, I was dripping in sweat. Mr. Hollon appeared to be dry and unfazed. I began to wonder which one of us was the 98-year-old in this equation. Needless to say, there was no way that I wanted to cut the tour of this backyard wonderland short.

"These are my Satsuma trees," he says, pointing to a couple of rather large trees, loaded with fruit. "They are like Mandarin oranges; easy to peel and delicious. That's where this town got its name from." Like the garden plants, the fruit on these trees was abundant and healthy, just a couple of months shy of ripening for harvest. Money doesn't grow on trees, I thought, but you sure do save you a lot of money at the grocery store with this kind of crop a short walk from your kitchen.

We made our way down to the boathouse on the edge of the creek. One gander at it, and there's no doubt that a fisherman has spent some quality time here. Mr. Hollon shared his love of fishing, along with a few 'big fish' tales, too. At just half his age, I'd surely struggle to conjure up the patience to fish for catfish, let alone muster up the physical strength and stamina to reel in a 30-pounder, but with his technique and years of experience, he pulls them right out of the water, cleans them up, and cooks them for dinner. "The thing about fishing," he says, "is you can give a man a fish and feed him a meal. I prefer to teach people how to fish, so they can feed themselves for life. That's what I've tried to do throughout my life, and that's what I want this book to accomplish."

I could taste the salt from the rivulet of sweat that was rolling down my cheek and into the corner of my mouth. Still unaffected by the heat, Mr. Hollon continued to regale me with fishing tales. I guess these conditions are a walk in the park for a man whose earliest memory in life is picking cotton on his family's Alabama farm. I was so enthralled with the conversation that I wiped my cheek, manned-up, and pushed on.

Our mutual interests, as well as the effortless ease of conversation between us, kept us in the backyard for the better part of an hour; however, the time flew by pleasantly. Had it not been for the heat, I could have spent all day in the yard with him.

As we made our way back up the incline toward the house, we passed the driveway and my truck. "I used to work in Detroit at the Ford plant," he remarked. "That didn't last long, but I do like their vehicles." I concurred as we finally headed into the house. A wave of cool, air-conditioned air welcomed me into the home, and so did his wife, Shirley Hollon. She is as charming and kind as her husband, and it was evident that they are smitten with each other. It's amazing how you can tell, just from an initial and brief interaction, that someone is having a great day. It appears that this couple hasn't had many, if any, bad days together.

Prior to my visit, I already knew that Mr. Hollon is a veteran because he shared that with me on our very first phone call, but photos on the wall of him in uniform invoked conversation about his service overseas during World War II. I would soon come to learn that he not only fought for freedom during the war, but he's also been a tenacious fighter his entire life. After all, he dedicated his business and spent his career fighting for financial independence and security for himself, his family, and his clients. Now, at the age of 98, he's still fighting for a better-managed, economically stable, fiscally responsible, debt-free country for his kids, grandkids, great grandkids, you and me, and generations to come.

He speaks with the pride and confidence that comes with knowing that his family is taken care of, not just because of the estate he has built, but, more importantly, because of the lessons he has taught them. Not everyone is lucky enough to have this man as their "Papa," but, thankfully, he is willing to share his wisdom with the world through this book.

Aside from enduring war-time combat action firsthand, Mr. Hollon has survived more than most people can imagine. His entry into the world came just three years before the Great Depression. He learned to be frugal, thrifty, productive and resourceful at an early age. These qualities certainly contributed to his tremendous success in business and money management. His tenacity, perseverance, care, conservative nature, and learned wisdom helped him survive many financial downturns, and shelter his clients' assets in the process. "My phone never rang during the downturns," he boasted multiple times; this being a testament to the fact that his clients have a great deal of trust in him. Even now, decades after he could have retired, he still has a burning desire to help others (and our country) prepare for and survive downturns and economic crises.

We sat down at the kitchen table and got right to business. It was immediately evident that he was prepared for this meeting. Neatly stacked folders full of articles, reports, statements, charts, and such were carefully placed on the table in order of importance. I noticed his impeccable handwriting on some of the folder tabs and the spreadsheets within them. The man was alert, focused, and articulate. He paused for emphasis after important points and maintained eye contact often. To say he was engaging would be a massive understatement. It was as if he had spent a lifetime preparing for this meeting. In fact, upon delving into the stacks of information, I quickly realized that what I was looking at was the culmination of this man's lifework.

It's crystal clear to anyone who will listen or observe, this man is driven by his passion for helping people live better lives. I could tell that the passion he has for gardening is the same as the burning passion he has for many other aspects of his life, including his career, his clients, his family and his wife.

Based on our conversations, and the empirical evidence and data he showed me at his kitchen table in the form of spreadsheets, charts, and financial statements to back up his claims, I can definitely surmise that he could have retired very comfortably a long time ago. Make no mistake, this man is actively and passionately working at his age, not because he has to, but because he truly wants to. He loves every minute of his work. I guess it's true; when you love what you do, you'll never work a day in your life. In fact, he's the oldest living financial advisor who is still actively working.

I had the pleasure of having lunch with Mr. and Mrs. Hollon at the local Cracker Barrel, a great choice for someone who is frugal, but loves southern comfort food. The restaurant never disappoints, and its consistency is one reason it's one of the Hollon's favorite dining locations. More impressive than the delicious food is this man's ability to get out and about at his age. For some, even decades younger, just putting on their socks is a challenge, but not Jim

Hollon, he still drives at 98! It's a big deal to have a business conversation with a 98-year-old man in a restaurant.

Not only did Mr. Hollon insist on paying for lunch, but he also demonstrated a tremendous amount of trust in me, and, rather than just paying me a deposit as called for in my author services agreement, he paid me in full, up front, for the entire project in lieu of four progress payments. Moreover, he did so on his own accord after emphasizing that he wanted this book completed as soon as possible. Most people in his position would leverage performance and speed by dangling the financial carrot in front of a service provider; however, Mr. Hollon leveraged my heart and my soul by placing so much trust in me. Nothing could have made me want to do right by him and this project more. This is a man you don't want to disappoint.

Trust is such an important element in business and in life. It should be treated as a treasure that must be respected and appreciated. It's not easily earned and can be lost in an instant. Trust is a foundation upon which Mr. Hollon has built his reputation, business, and legacy. He has been entrusted with the honor and responsibility of managing other peoples' money and large foundations' funds; more money than most of us would earn in a hundred lifetimes. That, to me, demonstrates a tremendous amount of trust earned, received, and retained. We will dive headfirst into the importance of trust much deeper as the story unfolds.

The love of family and friends, staying active, remaining up-to-date and relevant, giving of yourself, and following your purpose in life is all important to Mr. Hollon. Coupled with eating healthy by growing his own food, this level of good livin' is certainly a recipe for longevity. It's abundantly evident that this man has lived a long, happy, and fulfilled life. But he's not finished yet!...

If you are willing to read on, and really pay attention to the messages in his stories and embrace his strategies and ideas with an open mind, you might just learn a thing or two from this wise man. Who knows, you might change your life and achieve financial freedom. You may even end up helping to continue Mr. Hollon's goal and legacy of effecting positive change in this country and the world.

In the pages that follow, you will hear testimonials, examples, and success stories from many of Mr.

Hollon's peers and clients. Dr. Gordon Klingenschmitt, in his foreword, has already edified him for his patience, resolve, advanced thinking, and how he has been able to positively impact the finances of individuals and organizations by improving their efficiency and reducing risk. The good that he has done (and plans to continue doing) with the results of his efforts will undoubtedly solidify his world-changing legacy.

Dr. John VanValkenburg will later testify about how, with his advanced thinking, Mr. Hollon was able to solve a huge dilemma in the rules that applied to donations at the University where Dr. Van was employed. Not only did he help overcome this challenge in a positive way, but he also helped many other groups, including the Boy Scouts.

First and foremost, and without any further ado, you will read a heartfelt, humorous, entertaining, and analogous chapter by Charlton Hollon. It's a delightful read, and an insightful view into the life of James Hollon as experienced and recounted by his own grandson. Enjoy!

1

Reflections from a Grandson

Born in rural, southern Alabama in 1924, my paternal grandfather, James Ross Hollon ("Papa" to his grandchildren and great-grandchildren) is no stranger to hard work. In fact, he recalls his first childhood memory is that of being out in a field picking cotton. He also loved demonstrating the firmness of grip to us when we were young, a grip he attributed the result of all the years he had to milk the cows during his youth. Growing up on a farm simply required constant hard work. Raised during the Great Depression and having served in the military as a marine during World War II, my grandfather is a part of what Tom Brokaw famously termed "the greatest generation." For Papa, hard work has not only been a fact of life but a virtue he has embraced.

Shortly after returning home when the war ended, Papa decided to leave his hometown and travel to Detroit to see if he could work for Ford Motor Company. When he arrived, he saw a long line of applicants also looking for work. Someone, however, told him that when he made it to the person doing the interviews, he should make sure to say that he was from Alabama. Sure enough, when he got to the front of the line and mentioned his home state, they gave him a job because they figured this young man from the country would know how to work hard. Papa eventually ended up in the insurance business for many years, and then at an age when many begin thinking about resting in retirement, Papa began a new career (a process that in itself required a lot of hard work) and started working for himself as a financial advisor and coach. Although I am nearly forty years old, I have never known of a time that Papa was not working. In fact, at the time of this writing Papa is still working - at the age of ninety-eight!

While Papa clearly has no qualms about hard work, he has not been satisfied to simply work hard in life. Were that the case, I suppose he might have been content to remain working on his family farm or another job near his hometown. Instead, one of the central virtues I have seen Papa embody in his life is the importance of setting goals and then pursuing them by (as the old adage says) working *smart* and not just hard. The curiosity for things not yet known, the ability to think ahead and set challenging but achievable goals, the commitment to streamline one's efforts in order to more efficiently reach those goals; these are all qualities I have either heard about in family stories or witnessed as his grandson. In these few pages, I would like to offer my perspective on, and gratitude for, the lessons learned as his grandson.

I have very fond memories of visiting both sets of my grandparents as a child. While each side of my family was different, they both loved their grandchildren well. Graced with wonderful parents and grandparents, mine was a blessed childhood indeed. Going to visit Dad's parents, Papa and Bebe, as we called them, usually meant playing with toy cars (during my younger years), enjoying extra TV time, throwing the football in the front yard, or simply enjoying good conversation over delicious, southern-style meals. I recall pleasant memories of holidays with extended family, of conversation and laughter as old stories were told and retold - each telling never seeming to diminish the delight of the punchlines.

As children, we were allowed to play in just about any part of the house, with one notable exception: Papa's office. For good reason that room was simply off limits to us energetic grandchildren, so it was not often that I was allowed in. Perhaps due to its special "off limits" status, or perhaps due to the intrigue of all the binders, papers, and books that filled the space, his office carried the feeling of importance. Among the papers, binders and books, Papa also had little drawings, cartoons or sayings hanging up. One of these must have caught my attention because it made a lasting impression on me. It read simply: 'Think, maybe we can dodge some of this work."

Before considering its meaning, I find it noteworthy to observe the simple fact that he enjoyed collecting such sayings. His appreciation for little "common sense" sayings demonstrates something he has modeled for all his grandchildren, namely, the value of aphorisms. Learning pithy little sayings that encapsulate a truth in a memorable way allows for lessons to be easily memorized, utilized in various life situations and then easily passed on to others (as Papa did to his children and grandchildren). I do not ever remember Papa intentionally sitting us down when we were young and saying, "I'm going to tell you a list of sayings that will help you in life. Please memorize them." Instead, he simply repeated them over and over again in various situations because he enjoyed them himself. The result was that simply being around him meant we absorbed them naturally.

Think, maybe we can dodge some of this work.

This little saying in particular encapsulates for me a core ideal that I've seen Papa live out in a variety of ways, namely, the value of finding ways to work more efficiently and productively. At first glance, this little saying might seem to be encouraging laziness and irresponsibility. However, it encourages the possibility of avoiding *some* work, not all work. What kind of work is this advising us to avoid? At least as I saw it lived out in Papa's life, this saying meant attempting to avoid *unnecessary* work. In order to do that, the first step is to 'think,' that is, to analyze the task in front of you and the process you are considering using to accomplish it. Pausing to reflect on the task and your proposed solution will allow you to avoid wasted effort and inefficient methods.

Papa illustrated this aversion to inefficient work and unwillingness to make positive changes when those inefficiencies are identified by telling us the story of one of his first jobs after graduating from college. He went to work for a particular government agency and, to my knowledge, was tasked with managing the workflow and making things more productive.

He was not there long before he had identified redundancies and developed a plan on how to make the work more streamline. When the agency did not make changes Papa considered to be meaningfully helpful, he decided to look for work elsewhere.

A good insurance man finds the shade.

As previously mentioned, Papa worked in the insurance industry for many years. His role in the business required a lot of driving, whether that be in order to visit clients or in order to work with the agents he was managing. Heat being what it is in the South, getting back into a car that has been parked for any length of time outside in the sun is an unpleasant experience. Therefore, Papa learned the value of hunting for some shade to park in so that the car would not be as hot when he returned to it. For both my Dad and Papa, the idea that "a good insurance man finds the shade" became a saying that they often employed when parking the car for any reason. I have simply considered this a light-hearted little saying that got ensconced in our family vocabulary, but as I think about it now, this is another example of Papa using his analytical skills to make his work just a little more efficient and enjoyable. Hard work is necessary in life, but there are ways, sometimes as simple as parking in the shade, that can make the work a little less difficult or a little more efficient. A good insurance man - or someone in any profession - can likely identify a few small tricks to make the job a little easier.

Taking some leisure time to rejuvenate was another way Papa found to make his things a little easier. While he certainly worked hard, he also enjoyed the rest of fishing, in particular. This is a reminder to me of the need to "unplug' and be rejuvenated. As my Dad would say, sometimes you have to take time to sharpen the ax. No matter how hard you are willing to work at swinging a dull ax, it would be far better to take some time off from swinging to go and sharpen it. For Papa, he loved going fishing, and I have a hunch that this likely helped him "sharpen the ax."

Even in fishing, however, Papa's mind was still analyzing. While fishing usually called for more patience than I was prepared to give as a child, I do not remember ever feeling impatient due to remaining in the same spot for an extended amount of time if we were not getting results. Instead, fishing usually involved "hunting" for the fish. This meant looking at the terrain and foliage in order to find where he thought the fish were likely to be. Part of the analysis might also involve rethinking the type of bait we were using. He was, unsurprisingly, good at finding and catching them. If the fish were biting at all that day, Papa could usually help us get a "mess" of them. As one might expect, fishing came with its own set of sayings. "You can't catch fish on credit" was a way of reminding us to check our bait and make sure we were not fishing with an empty hook after some clever fish had managed to nibble off the bait. Fishing on an empty hook would be a lot of wasted effort and a little awareness to check on your bait occasionally would help a good fisherman dodge that.

These times of relaxation are fond memories for me as I recall not only the fishing, but also taking our "mess" of fish back to the house, watching him clean them and then fry them. The delicious meal usually involved hush puppies he fried along with the fish, some fresh vegetables from his garden, and (my personal favorite), homemade peach ice cream. While all of the gardening, fishing and cooking required hard work, this was the kind of work you would not want to dodge. Hard work is a part of life, but there are activities that can make it more enjoyable, whether that be finding the shade or finding the fish.

Don't let the seeds get in the way of enjoying the watermelon.

Another fond memory I have of going to Papa and Bebe's house is eating watermelon on their back deck. The cool, sweet watermelon was a welcome treat on warm summer evenings. While the watermelon itself was good, it would be easy, especially for a child, to be annoyed by the seeds. Instead of complaining about the seeds, I remember enjoying them because Papa taught us how to "shoot" the watermelon seeds with our fingers. Instead of the seeds being an annoyance, he had turned them into a fun aspect of the experience. Years later, Papa told me, "Don't let the seeds get in the way of enjoying the watermelon," thus reminding me about the importance of gratitude. It would be a shame to allow the difficulties or annoyances in life to keep you from enjoying the blessings.

The importance of gratitude was further reinforced by a common remark Papa made as he would sit down to a meal. Even though many times he was the one who had cooked a good bit of the meal, he would sit down and say, "Sure am glad I could come!" This demonstrated the importance of gratitude; a way of reminding oneself that we ought not take the blessings of life that God gives us for granted. Papa's experience of growing up during the Great Depression likely helped him not take things like a good meal for granted, and his example was a good reminder to his grandchildren that we should also cultivate gratitude in life, even if we have to look past a few watermelon seeds.

Shake it off and step up!

While we want to cultivate an attitude of gratitude, there are inevitable challenges in life that are definitely larger than the small "watermelon seed" annoyances. In the face of these life challenges, Papa is fond of telling a story about an old mule that fell into a pit. At first it seemed impossible that the mule would ever be able to get out since he was obviously unable to climb.

Presently, however, as the farmer began to shovel dirt into the pit on top of the mule, the resourceful animal would simply shake off the dirt and step up onto the now slightly higher ground. This process of shaking the incoming dirt off and stepping up onto it repeated itself until the mule simply walked out of the pit. Papa told this story to teach his grandchildren the value of perseverance and resourcefulness in the face of challenges.

What seems to be the difficulty?

Of course, some of the challenges we face in life are a result of our own making. My Dad and his younger brother are fond of retelling a parenting technique Papa employed to remind his children of their responsibility to behave. As the story goes, when my dad and his younger brother would be acting up in some way and Papa found out about it, he would approach them with the firm question, "What seems to be the difficulty?" The implication was that there should be no difficulty. Someone had made, or was making, a poor decision that was causing the difficulty, and they needed to cease and desist immediately. A standard of acceptable behavior was expected to be followed, and when that was not followed, there would be consequences. I not only had the blessing of being raised with similar expectations, but now, as I hear my own children begin to get upset at one another or become otherwise unruly, I've been known to head towards them asking, 'What seems to be the difficulty?' The expectation is that there will not only cease to be a difficulty, but that they might consider refraining from such difficulty in the future.

Raisins in the squash?

When I was in my teen years and my grandmother became too ill to cook, Papa took over the cooking responsibilities for family get-togethers. While I did not pay close attention to the activity in the kitchen, I do not remember Papa being one to read and carefully follow recipes. Instead, he seemed to enjoy experimenting. It was an example of what I also saw him attempt in his work - valuing curiosity and thinking outside the box. One humorous story that reminds me of Papa's penchant for out of the box thinking was his decision to cook squash and add raisins to it. When the meal was served, someone, surprised, asked about the raisins in the squash. I think Papa enjoyed the question and the chance to comment on his new experiment. Raisins in the squash became a short-hand way of remembering Papa's innovative thinking. While outside the box thinking certainly helped Papa solve problems in his work, it also meant we got to try some new ideas. And, in case anyone is curious, raisins are not too bad in squash.

I've been blessed to grow up listening, watching and learning from Papa. He is incessantly curious, constantly working toward new goals and seeking to pass on lessons learned along the way to his children and grandchildren. There was seldom a hunting trip or long conversation over a meal without him teaching some lesson or imparting some wisdom. I have had the blessing of seeing Papa's wisdom lived out in average daily tasks of life as well as the fun activities of hunting, fishing and storytelling. He has always been a hard worker, but also is always on the lookout for a better way of doing something. After all, if you think, you might be able to dodge some unnecessary work.

Charlton Ross Hollon
July 2022
Birmingham, Alabama

2
Who is James R. Hollon?

First and foremost, before I formally introduce myself and delve into my personal history, if you didn't read Dr. Gordon Klingenschmitt's foreword and the ghostwriter's preface, "Meeting Mr. Hollon," I highly recommend you go back and do so right now. There's important information in both.

I would like to emphatically state my intentions for this book. I'm not looking for any new clients, or to make money off this book venture. My vision is for this book to effect positive change in the world; by reducing our country's debt and improving our snowballing financial dilemma; by eliminating waste and reducing risk so that foundations can be more profitable; by educating you in a way that positively impacts your personal finances and wealth accumulation; and by creating fiscally responsible strategies that leave this world a better place for future generations. My intention is to share what I've learned by working with 501(c)3 foundations throughout my career. I have a tremendous amount of experience and wisdom in this area; real, solid, tried and true information that should be very valuable to you.

With that being said, please allow me to introduce myself...

I'm James R. Hollon, but many of my friends, family, colleagues, and clients call me Jim. I was born on July 5th, 1924, in the city of Headland, Alabama. I'm a junior, as my father was James R. Hollon, Sr. My paternal grandparents were already deceased by the time I was born, so I never got to meet them. My mother, Beatrice Louise Smith, was born in Baker Hill, Alabama. My maternal grandparents, Anderson and Magnolia Smith, were still living, and I had the pleasure of spending time with them while I was growing up.

I have four siblings: an older sister, Ferell; a younger sister, Virginia; a younger brother, Felix Scott; and a baby sister, Nancy, who is still alive today. My other siblings are all deceased.

Ferell graduated from high school, then jumped on a train to Washington DC and went to work at the Pentagon, never to return to the south. Virginia's husband was a paper-making machine repairman, and his career took them to various places. Felix

Scott was a salesman and insurance man like me. After a bit of convincing, I finally got him away from the company he was with and over to the company I was with. He had bypass surgery in 1986, and subsequently went on disability. Nancy still lives in Corpus Christi, Texas. She married an Air Force man but got divorced. She later married a head-shrinker, and she got her degree in psychology.

My very first memory is from 93 years ago, when I was five years old. We lived in a house on the corner of Hollon Street and Cleveland Avenue. Back then, residents could name the streets they lived on. My granddaddy Hollon homesteaded four houses on Hollon Street, four 40-acre lots (one for each of the kids), plus another 55-acre plot, which began the Hollon history in Headland, Alabama. When I was five, our home burned down. Dad was a butcher in a local grocery store at the time, but he got an advance to buy a 100-acre farm in Headland. I grew up working on the farm from the time I was five. We grew cotton, corn, and peanuts as cash crops, and we had a one-acre garden in which we grew our own vegetables. We also had our own livestock, including a cow I milked every morning. Then, in 1941, the government leased our farmland and turned it into an airport landing strip. Two years later, they condemned it for public domain and took permanent possession of it. Much to my chagrin, my father bought another, even larger farm, which I also worked.

Technically, I never finished high school, but there's a story. In 1942, I lacked 2½ course credits, so I went to the principal of Henry County High School and asked him if I could take enough courses in summer school to graduate. He said I could only take a maximum of two courses in summer school, but he told me if I kept the shrubbery trimmed and the grounds tidy at the school campus and the agriculture building, he'd sign off for me to graduate. It made sense because I was already involved in agriculture studies in school, plus I had plenty of experience tending to the family farm. So, that's what I did. I walked three miles each way to school and back home every day, I kept the school grounds pristine, and I graduated.

In 1944, I was drafted into the Marines. This afforded me a reprieve from farming but left the farm unkempt during my absence. Dad was a disabled World War 1 Army veteran who served in France. He got gassed in the war and had many health complications from it; therefore, he could not farm himself. He was, however, a good supervisor. His prior experience as a supervisor in a peanut and cottonseed mill prepared him for that role.

After serving in the Pacific theater during WWII as a machine gunner, my military service ended in January of 1946. I immediately went back to farming the 320-acre farm, and I soon got it back into cultivation. In October of the same year, I told my father that I would not farm next year. I informed him I would be permanently retiring from farm work. It was not paying me anything except room and board anyway. It was tough work, and I was through with it. As a result, Dad decided to sell the farm, which was located in the panhandle of Florida, and move back to Alabama. And that is what he ultimately did.

My decision to leave the farm began a new chapter in my life.

On January 7th, 1947, I rode the Greyhound bus from Alabama to Detroit, Michigan, in search of an industrial job. Luck was with me, and, upon my arrival, I found a job the very next day at Ford Motor Company in their Highland Park plant. Maybe it was luck, or maybe it was the result of proper prior planning, coupled with some insider information. I was told in advance that, even if the employment line was two blocks long, to get in it and stay in it until I got through the door. I was further instructed to make sure that, if asked, I tell the interviewer I was from Alabama, which I did. Alabama farmers had a reputation for being very hard workers. Plus, I was wearing my green Marines jacket, which, being from the South, was the only article of clothing I owned that was appropriate for January weather in Detroit. Anyway, they put me to work the very same day! I worked six months on the assembly line building Ford 2½-ton trucks. During my time at Ford, I observed and learned. I studied how they did things and the systems and strategies they used on the assembly line. After all, it was Ford, one of the most successful manufacturing companies in the world. That was probably my ulterior motive for wanting to work there in the first place. My advanced thinking had directed me to prepare myself for industrial work as an alternative to farming.

Inspired by what I learned at Ford, and with a GI bill in my hip pocket as a result of my military service, I decided to return to Alabama and apply to Auburn University in pursuit of a degree in industrial management. I couldn't get into the summer term at Auburn, but I did get accepted into the fall semester. In the meantime, I drove a truck for the state prison facility, hauling prisoners up and down the road. It was a temporary but "interesting" job, and it paid my bills until I started college in September.

Three years later, in August of 1950, I received my degree in industrial management. While pursuing my degree, I also studied corporation structure and what jobs were available therein. Incidentally, I decided to take two electives: property and casualty insurance, and life insurance courses. My advanced thinking led me to believe that these courses would benefit me in almost any management job. I knew that if I ended up in a big manufacturing company at some point, this information would possibly allow me to work in that area of the company, rather than on the assembly line. To my pleasant surprise, I fell in love with the life insurance business.

My first job after college was working in the management office of the Anniston Alabama Army Depot. One of my jobs was to study systems, flow charts, documents, and such at the depot. It didn't take me long to discover that 21 people were all filing unneeded, duplicate copies of the same document. There was no need for the additional documents, so I essentially eliminated 21 peoples' jobs. This revealed my ability to cut waste early in my professional life. When I pointed this waste of human effort out to the leadership there, they simply shuffled those 21 workers into other positions. No one lost their job, though.

Now, you can imagine my thoughts. That's when my attitude towards government work began to deteriorate and my advanced thinking killed my enthusiasm for government management office work. This invoked more thought about making positive changes for myself.

My last duty at Anniston was to study the use of forms in the entire depot. I convinced them to buy a typewriter and hire someone who knew how to type. I collected copies of all the forms that were in use at the depot, and I designed new forms. I created a system so that when you put the form into the typewriter and lined up the first line, all someone had to do was click the lever to move to the next item. The typewriter carriage went to the right place, so you didn't have to adjust the typewriter anymore. Many of you who are reading this book today will never understand the trials and tribulations associated with typing on a manual typewriter. Because of that endeavor, the colonel of the depot wrote me a letter of recommendation.

My job at the Anniston Army Depot lasted a total of about two-and-half years. While I was at the depot, I had learned to sell life insurance part time while working at my management job in the daytime. I managed to lead the office in sales four out of the five years I was there. Soon, my pay was equal between the management job and insurance sales. This spawned more advanced thinking.

At that time in my life, things were popping, and even more things were to happen. On June 8th, 1948, I married my grade school sweetheart, Betty Espy, who I met while attending Headland High School. We ended up having three sons: Tom Robert Hollon, born 5/31/51; James Herbert Hollon, born 6/10/55; and Kim Norton Hollon, born 8/9/57.

My life insurance sales earnings paid the hospital bill for my first son's birth. This gave me the confidence to consider selling full time. My "future thinking" took over and was driving me to totally change direction. It became very important to me to "discover myself" and make the decision to do what I was really good at. Second, I really wanted to help people and maybe even make a good living for my new family. Thus, my interest in my job at the Anniston Army Depot became second in thought.

A salesman who was calling on me while I was at the depot kept trying to recruit me to sell multilith machines and reproducing machines in Birmingham. I gave it serious thought, and even went to Birmingham job hunting and to further explore the opportunity, but I did not think it was of enough interest to keep me fulfilled and in lifetime work. So, I had no interest there, and declined the position; however, my passion to change careers kept pressing me.

In my first year at Liberty National Life, I made $10,000, less expenses, in just nine months, whereas I had been making only $2,005 per year at the depot. It was a very good "raise" and a whole lot of money at the time. This really put my career in life insurance on the right path. I could do work that helped people and be paid decently for it. Guess what?... Anniston Army Depot offered me $2,250 to stay with them. I thanked them for the offer, but I left. I was ready to begin my new career. Things were moving on and big changes were about to unfold for me.

When I made the decision to change careers, it was a big deal because I had a lot of mouths to feed. This helped put pressure on me to do even better at life insurance sales. So, I decided to go full-time in the insurance business.

Advanced thinking took me to Orlando, Florida, job hunting, and I quickly found a job with Metropolitan Life Insurance in Leesburg, Florida. After the interview, I returned to Birmingham and decided to leave Liberty National Life Insurance and move to Florida. I informed Liberty of my decision, and they called me into the Birmingham office for talks. The manager gave me a test and I did excellent on it. He told me to come back and meet a sales manager, which I did on Saturday morning. The meeting went well, and my career and job for the next 28 ½ years was set.

The vice president of Liberty at the time, Al Biggio, called the Orlando manager, Frank Rafoni, and told him to create a job for me there. I decided to take that newly created position in order to get established in Orlando. My work there lasted only nine weeks before I was offered a management job as a sales manager in Atlanta under the same sales manager who had originally hired me full-time with Liberty. That brought things full circle, so to speak.

I learned a lot during the time I worked under my old boss and the sales manager there. I learned how to do things the right way, and I also learned what not to do as well. The boss and sales manager got drunk at a party once. The sales manager stayed drunk for an entire week, so the boss demoted him to agent again. So, the agent became a sore head in the office. Eventually, both of them were removed from Atlanta and relocated elsewhere.

A new manager arrived, and I continued to work there for about two more years until Betty, my wife, got sick with an ulcer between her stomach and small intestine. This burdened us with high medical and drug bills, so after working in Atlanta for about 4½ years, I requested to be transferred to Piedmont, Alabama in order to make more money. This was a good move and a much better environment for my family.

After a few years, I was transferred back to Birmingham in the Woodlawn district office for one year as the fifth sales manager there. They knew I was a hard worker and they wanted me to crack the whip on the other four managers in that office. I went right to work on that request, and I was soon promoted to manager and assigned to open a new district office in Lafayette, Georgia for a two-year stint there. After that, I was sent to Memphis, Tennessee, for ten months to open an office there, close to Elvis Presley's place. Meanwhile, in Memphis, Martin Luther King had just been killed and everything was in chaos there. I needed to get my three boys back into good schools, so I asked to be moved back to Birmingham to the Woodlawn office as the sales manager. This worked for the company, as well as my family, and we moved into the Mountain Brook school district.

In December of 1970, I was promoted again to manage the Montevallo district office. The Montevallo district had never been a producing district until I started there. I qualified to make the company convention (a high honor) every year for 11 out of the 12 years I was the manager there. My first year there was the only year that I did not qualify. Overall, I would make the company convention 23 out of the 28 years I was at Liberty National Life.

Life was good. I was working in a career I loved, and I was making good money at it. Plus, I really developed a penchant for helping people. It was my desire to do good for others that led me to explore and join some extracurricular organizations. I became a Freemason in 1948. The Masonic order is a secret organization, and they don't advertise or go out looking for members. My grandfather on my mother's side was a Mason. I always looked up to my granddaddy, and I liked everything he did. So, curiosity got the best of me, and I asked a friend how I could become part of the Masonic Order. He became my liaison into the organization. Then, in 1964, I became a Shriner as well. The Shriners do a lot of work to help children who need medical attention; that's what drove me to participate in that organization.

Now back to my career at Liberty. The market had evolved over the years, but the company would not make any efforts to improve their products. My advanced thinking led me to plan and prepare for a departure from Liberty. I ordered all the certified financial planner books I would need to study in order to take the CFP exams. When I finished putting in a full week of work at my job on Friday evenings, I would then start reading and studying, all weekend long, day and night, for three years. All the while, I was still maintaining a first-class office at Liberty.

The CFP study of all the big investment books, planning books, insurance books, etc. took me three solid years while I was still performing my managerial job.

In January of 1981, I passed all five CFP exams and was finally able to execute my plan. I was more than ready to sell securities! So, on August 31st, 1981, after 28 years of loyal and faithful service, I put in my notice with Liberty and quit. At the time, I was managing seventeen agents, two sales managers, and four ladies who were administrative assistants running the office. My entrepreneurial mindset and advanced thinking told me that Liberty wasn't going to keep me employed past the age of 65 anyway. Forced retirement was the reality I was facing. With only eight years left before that would happen, I knew I had a lot more to give, and a lot more to earn before I retired. Plus, I fell in love with my career, and had no intention of retiring anytime soon.

This is when I finally started working for myself.

I founded my very first business, J.R. Hollon & Associates, Inc., a C-Corp, on August 31st, 1981. That same corporation is still in business today, and it will survive me and transfer to my three sons, who are more than capable of running it.

It took a lot of fortitude to quit my job at the age of 57 without having a paycheck to replace it. Now let's see if I had the courage to make my future thinking work. Well, it's 41 years later, and I still haven't retired. I'm still actively working, by choice, not necessity, as a financial advisor for an Alabama foundation and a large testamentary trust, and I'm a foundation consultant with close to nearly $100 million under management, which includes my clients and myself.

Throughout my career, I've helped clients balance their portfolios, minimize their risk and increase their returns. I charge no hidden fees and I create a tax shelter for my clients.

Why am I still actively working today? I can sum it up in one word: PASSION. I definitely don't need to work at my age, but I choose to continue to do so. I want to make a lasting impression. My kids, grandkids, and great grandkids are all taken care of, but what about the rest of the world around them? I still have a burning desire and a passion for helping people achieve financial freedom and live better lives as a result.

This book can impact you, your family, your business, foundations, non-profits, and our country as a whole. When these strategies are implemented, everyone wins.

Longevity is possible; I'm proof of that. Don't outlive your wealth, that's important. I have no financial worries - neither does my family. The stability and security I enjoy has been achieved directly from the strategies I'm sharing with you in this book. Read on, you just might learn something profound and beneficial.

So, how do I stack up in regard to being the oldest working financial advisor in the USA? Well, the second oldest actively working CFP that I could find on the internet is 93 years old. At 98, I'm still not finished yet. In fact, this is the time when I really get busy...

3
The Problem

Okay, dear reader, I have a few questions for you to ponder:

- Would you say that the United States is in a better position financially now than it was 5, 10, or even 50 years ago?
- Are the cost of goods and services currently going up or down?
- Would you say that our government is fiscally responsible?
- Is our national debt increasing or decreasing?
  - Is there any hope in sight for us to curtail and pay off the national debt?
  - If so, how do you think it could or should happen?
- Do you think the government will drastically raise taxes at some point in the future?
- Did you know that we are on the verge of yet another government shutdown unless we raise the debt ceiling again?
- Do you think that our economy is heading in the right direction?

- Would you say that the average American and their family is prepared for continued inflation and/or eventual retirement?
- Is the average American even financially prepared for a minor setback like an automobile repair, or worse, a "real emergency" such as a health crisis, layoff or divorce?

According to Google, in 2019 (pre-COVID) the average American adult had $6,271 in individual credit card debt. In 2021, the average American household debt was $96,371. It's quite obvious that most Americans are borrowing just to survive.

The government is also borrowing money to keep the country afloat. The national debt has steadily increased every year over the past ten years. The national debt surpassed $31 trillion in 2022. That's $2.5 trillion more than it was in 2021! As of August 2022, it costs roughly $678 billion just to maintain the national debt. That figure is 13% of the total federal spending. This is creating a growing and unsustainable tax burden for future generations.

More and more baby boomers are retiring and collecting social security. People are living longer, which is good; however, it's burdening the system.

Many younger generations wonder if there will be any money left in the social security system by the time they retire, yet they do little, if anything, to prepare for such a conundrum.

To make matters worse, post-COVID, the United States has experienced some of the most drastic inflation the country has seen in decades. The cost of food, fuel, housing, and other necessities is rapidly becoming unaffordable for many low-income and even middle-class families. This situation will certainly put a greater burden on our welfare system and government subsidy programs. Where will that money come from? You guessed it - higher debt, and, ultimately, more taxes.

It is my belief that most of our financial problems today are a direct result of waste and mismanagement of funds on almost every level - from the top of the government, right down to our households and the individuals therein.

So, what's the solution? I'm glad you asked...

4
The Plan

Failing to plan is planning to fail. Have a plan for your future.

Sometimes, the solutions to complex problems can be quite simple. Oftentimes, we overcomplicate things and "make mountains out of molehills." Furthermore, solutions can be overlooked because they are right under your nose. It's my goal to cut through all the nonsense and discuss some simple, effective solutions to complex problems that have been brewing for quite some time.

What I plan to cover over the next chapters in this book, if you'll stay with me, is to lay out a simple, easily understandable plan that foundations can follow to cut costs, minimize risk, eliminate the need for fundraising, and increase returns. If you pay close attention to my strategies, you just might discover that many of these principles could be well-applied to your business and personal life as well.

Before we get into all of that, I want to convey the importance of identifying your problems. It's near impossible to create an effective and efficient plan until you have identified what issues are causing you the greatest challenges.

If I were to sit down with you for a consultation, I would use the following list of questions to identify and prioritize your financial situation. In order to determine if your portfolio is broken, and, if so, how to fix it, give the following questions a read. Then read the questions again, and this time take the time to answer each one honestly and thoroughly. You just might learn some things about yourself and create the beginnings of a personal financial plan in the process.

1. If I had a magic wand, what are the biggest problems that I could solve in your current financial situation?

    1. _____

    2. _____

    3. _____

2. How much do you estimate each problem is costing you in dollars?

    1. $_____

    2. $_____

    3. $_____

3. If these problems go unsolved, how much do you think it will cost you, cumulatively, over the next five years? $_____

4. How long have you had these problems?

    1. _____

    2. _____

    3. _____

5. How long have you tried to fix them?

    1. _____

    2. _____

    3. _____

6. How has your planner or advisor tried to fix them? _____

7. Do these problems affect anyone else? _____

8. Are these problems important? _____

9. Imagine yourself five years in the future and none of these problems have been solved. In one word how would you feel? _____

10. How much have you budgeted to solve these problems? (Time, Energy, Focus, Money) _____

11. Peace of mind meter: On a scale of one to ten, rate your peace of mind around your investments, finances, and taxes.

12. Are you currently working with a financial planner or advisor?
13. Have you ever received a written financial plan?
14. How many other planners or advisors have you worked with? _____
15. What is the most frustrating thing about the planning process you are now using?
16. Have you ever had an independent analysis done on your portfolio? _____
17. Is it important to you to control risk in your portfolio? _____
18. Do you have a scientific method for measuring risk in your portfolio and do you know what this number is? _____
19. Can you control something you cannot measure? _____
20. Is diversification important to you? _____
21. Do you know how to measure diversification?

_____

22. Has anyone ever calculated the hidden internal cost in your investment portfolio?

_____

23. Do you know the yearly average turnover of the mutual funds in your portfolio?

_____

24. Do you have an investment policy statement?
_____

25. Do your existing planners/advisors primarily work on a fee or commission basis? _____

26. Do they provide you with a quarterly statement summarizing all of their commissions and costs or do they hide most of them? _____

27. Do you know what the expected historic rate of return is for the mix of assets you now possess? _____

28. Do you know how much you could lose over a two to three-year market crash? In other words, what is the historic worst-case scenario for your current mix?

_____

Now that you have answered these questions, we can move on and begin to improve your financial situation.

In the next chapter, I will discuss change and its prevalence and importance. Then we will tackle the fundamentals of a decades-old Nobel prize winning financial strategy as well as modern portfolio principles. We will explore ways to convert waste into benefit. You'll discover that small moves, over time, can produce big results. Other advanced thinker strategies will also be employed to reduce risk and maximize returns.

Of course, there'll be some stories, and probably a few aphorisms mixed in here as well. After all, facts tell, but stories sell. Few people will remember the facts, but most people will remember a good story and the lessons therein.

5

Nails, Hot Water, Toasters, and Change

If you continue to do what you've always done, you'll get what you've always gotten. Maybe. Or, sometimes, what's worked in the past will cease to work in the future as the world changes and evolves around us. No one is buying stock in Kodak today.

Change, as defined by Merriam Webster's dictionary, is:
(verb)

> a: to make different in some particular: ALTER
> b: to make radically different: TRANSFORM
> c: to give a different position, course, or direction

I'd like to think that my advanced thinking and future thinking strategies have made me a pioneer in regard to change. Sadly, if only more of my 'prospective' clients had been willing to embrace change, they could have joined the ranks of my clients who now enjoy financial freedom.

So, why are most people so resistant to change? Could comfort be the culprit?

To illustrate my point, I'd like to share a story. You may have heard a version of it before, but I call this version "nailed it," because it really hits the nail on the head in regard to many people's mindset nowadays.

Little Johnny went to the country to visit his Granpaw who was sittin' on the front porch smokin' his pipe in his rockin' chair. His old blue tick hound was sittin' next to him just a howlin' up a storm.

"Howwooh, arrrr, howwooh," the hound hollered as his ears dangled when he threw his head back to let out his guttural bellow.

Granpaw just kept rockin' away as a trail of smoke rose from the pipe that hung loosely from his lip. He seemed to pay no mind to the fact that the dog was hollerin' right next to him.

"Howwooh, arrrr, howwooh," the hound continued every few seconds or so - causin' lil Johnny to wince with aggravation from the annoyin' sound every time.

Finally, outta curiosity, lil Johnny asked, "Granpaw, why is your dog hollerin' so bad?"

Granpaw continued rockin' as he reached up and removed the smokin' pipe from his lip long enough to reply in his southern drawl, "He's sittin' on a nail."

Lil Johnny seemed perplexed and mulled over the situation for a bit as the dog kept on hollerin' and Granpaw just kept on rockin'.

"Well, why doesn't he just move, Granpaw?"

Granpaw cut his eyes down to the hollerin' hound as he once again pulled the pipe from his mouth to respond, "Well, I reckon it don't hurt him bad enough."

Do you ever find yourself sitting on a metaphorical nail? Maybe it's working a job you hate, failing to balance your checkbook, or settling for sub-par effort from yourself. What's your nail? What's causing you discomfort in life?

Not all of us are sitting on nails; some of us are in hot water. If you throw a frog into boiling water, he'll jump right out, but if you put him in a pot of room temperature water and gradually raise the temperature one degree or so every few minutes, you'll boil him, and he'll never feel it coming. Many people think they're relaxing in a hot tub, but it just ain't so. This country, and many of its foundations, non-profits, businesses, and individuals are in hot water right now, on the verge of boiling! What's your temperature and appetite for change?

The bad news is, nothing in your life is likely to change for the positive unless you're willing to get up off your tail and take action to make positive change. The good news is that you can change most any aspect of your life with one split second of positive and decisive thought. This thought will ignite emotions and invoke positive actions that will propel you closer to that which you truly want in life.

So, what does it really take to make a man want to change? A newspaper study once revealed that 41% of people will not change for any reason, but if a bank is offering them a new toaster as an incentive, they will move their assets in a heartbeat! Are you currently sitting on your assets, even if they are remaining idle?

If you're not changing, you're probably dying. If your money is sitting idle, it just got a sizable haircut due to inflation over the last couple of years. Don't let your hard-earned money wither and die.

My advanced thinking fuels my burning desire to achieve superior performance in all of my endeavors. Years ago, I brought a new financial concept to Alabama clients. Just think for a moment, no one was offering this concept yet, especially in Alabama. So, can you imagine what a hard sell it was? Now, even after decades of data, countless success stories, client testimonials, and with all the progress I have personally made, it still blows my mind that people do not want to change. I guess, like life, you find new curiosities to distract you. If they're interesting enough, I reckon sometimes they move you in a direction to explore them further.

What a trying time America is going through right now. Isn't it time for some change? Is it time to consider our present, our past, and our future direction? Can we unify our country back together in order to keep our country's free markets working, and our freedom established forever? Should we think about someone telling us what we can and can't do? Will this not cause you to think about when the rubber hits the road? Let's do some evaluation of situations in our present that might be cause for serious concern.

First and foremost, our economy is in shambles, would you agree? What seems to be the problem? Could it be due to some rapid changes that occurred without any planning, without any set goals for accomplishment for our country? Then ask, how do you get other countries to do the same? Is it fair to ask what the ultimate total cost to our country, our businesses, and our individuals will be? Can we ask what proof we have that such total change, all at once, will prove to change anything? So, would you agree that the cost of this change is prohibitive to the economy? Are there other causes for concern?

What about taxes, doesn't someone have to pay the price for this change? Taxes, taxes, and more taxes are being levied against businesses as well as individuals. What does this cause? The results are evident in the form of high inflation, a recession, loss of jobs, foreclosures, auto repossessions, apartment evictions, and possible food shortages. What about the national deficit? Is it possible that our country will stay divided, and things will get worse with more questionable changes coming? Is there a more serious concern?

Freedom, freedom, freedom - who wants to give it up? Do you want all of the changes that have been made so far, and the ones that can be made in the future, to lead us straight into socialism? If you study some of the socialist countries in the world, is it safe to say that some, if not most, are in misery? Haven't our forefathers worked diligently and super hard to guide America to become a great nation of freedom? Wouldn't the earliest settlers of America be very proud of our past history and our ability to remain free so far? What other serious concerns are there?

I would like to quote Dr. Iben Browning's remarks, which were made in a presentation to the National Association of Financial Planners in 1980's annual meeting. He said, "Man could not throw up enough bad stuff, up in the air, and keep it there to affect our weather." May we ask, if man changes the climate, what assurance do we have that it won't be worse than it is today? Another quote from Dr. Browning is, "The high tides cause the earth plates to move, which would cause volcanoes to erupt, throwing so much pollution into the air, thus causing famines, wherever the cloud moved, for about five years." What would this situation contribute to climate change? I would like to know what caused the last ice age so many years ago, before we had to own only electric vehicles.

Who will benefit from the stocks of all of the businesses that will bring about all of these changes? Who knows how many will fail, and how many individuals will end up owning worthless stock or bonds? Will there be any stopping these changes, should things get worse than they are in our present?

Aren't there vibrations which indicate that all the mass changes of our present haven't been exposed? Who knows what is next? Surely, you and I know the future changes will be even more unsettling. Do we have enough people concerned that effort will be put forth to help stop the problem and correct it? Is there more to be exposed?

Our broad tax structure is so complicated that we need to add 87,000 new employees to the IRS payroll. Can we all agree that everything that has ever been given any thought has been taxed? Is it possible to scrap the current system and come up with a simple tax that people will honor and pay their fair share? I think so. Now, let's give some serious thought about what the total cost of implementing the current system is; the cost to the IRS, businesses, individuals, CPA's, tax preparers, non-profits, foundations, and universities - the list could go on and on.

Just look at the hidden costs a billion-dollar foundation within a university has in regard to complying with IRS rules, just to pass muster. Quoting from Google, "These four institutions' endowments increased in value from 127.4 billion to 171 billion in one year. The current rankings of the three largest foundations by total assets are as follows:

1. Thrivent Financial, $109,548,684,484
2. Fairbanks Etelsen, $95,328,000,000
3. Welcome Trust, $42,269,400,000
4. Google shows the next 100 largest endowment funds.

Now look at what the total assets of the following 501(c)3s could possibly be: endowments, foundations, non-profits, etc. Imagine what the operating costs of a billion-dollar foundation are for just one year. Now let's add the cost of operating affiliated foundations, transaction costs of investing one billion dollars for a year, expense ratio of funds owned, sales charges, turnover, hidden costs of funds, employees to carry on operations, health care cost for employees, pension cost for employees, costs paid to board members, fees to advisors, costs to have a bold investment committee, a special employee or employees to handle buying and selling stocks and bonds, CPA's cost and more. The list goes on.

So, can we compare the cost of operating a foundation where all the assets are in an asset allocation plan, like that of the Nobel Prize for Economics in 1990? Almost all of the costs are eliminated. The average grant for the first 20 years of operations, without any fundraising or adding to corpus was an outstanding 8.39%. Along with this, their fiduciary responsibility was transferred to the money manager of the asset allocation plan, thus saving insurance cost, also. What else do we want to think about in the way of cost of operations? You will find a total list of 20 costs that can possibly be eliminated in an article later on.

Most large foundations or university foundations have big philanthropy departments in their operations. Isn't this how they keep growing the foundations? Why even think about this? Does the foundation have to run assets through their cost structure with all the other assets? Can we question that and look at another way to handle philanthropy gifts and eliminate the foundation cost? May I suggest that all philanthropy gifts go directly to the charity of the donors if the donor is seeking a tax donation. This may seem wild, but costs have to be cut drastically.

At my age, I have dealt with both our present and our past history. So, may I deal with the future for a moment now? May I give you a reason to care, and possibly even change?

Suppose we use the rule of 72, and say an employee is making $100,000 per year and inflation is 10%. By dividing 10% interest into 72, the rule of 72 tells us that an employee's earnings should be $200,000 in 7.2 years just to keep up with inflation alone. No one knows this. It prompts me to ask, how can we get all political parties to become conservatives? Our leaders should not pass any laws without considering cost, period.

Our present, our past, and our future do not have to be the same. We all should have learned by now that we can change. Wouldn't you agree that we need to do something about our present and our future? What you tell yourself is likely to be what happens.

Life is precious. We only get one life to live, and every minute we waste is precious time that can never be regained; time that could have (and should have) been spent focusing on taking action toward the solution. Let's take some action...

6

Sailing Over the Mountain

Now, for one of my greatest curiosities...

My first wife, Betty, died in 2010 after a courageous battle with cancer. A year later, on June 11, 2011, I married my second and current wife, Shirley. Shirley and I honeymooned in Italy for 17 days, from Rome down the coast and around the boot and back. Prior to my honeymoon, I had already been to Italy twice for conventions. I really enjoy traveling.

At some point later, I learned, as a result of my many readings, that there was a ship somewhere in Europe that sailed over mountains. This was very interesting to me, and I wondered how someone came up with the thought to make this possible. Who was this advanced thinker and how did he achieve this monumental feat?

Curiosity got the best of me, so I decided to go back to Europe just to experience this incredible trip. Shirley and I flew to Budapest and boarded the ship. Fifteen days later, we were in Amsterdam. We traveled through three different rivers and over 100 different locks, which changed the elevation of the ship throughout the waterways. The scenery was surreal as we literally sailed over the mountains!

If that is not enough, think about traveling through seven different countries to get to the end destination. Furthermore, imagine the daily side trips into these seven countries. You get to see and experience firsthand the different customs, art, and culture in each area you travel into. You even get to enjoy unique cuisines and beverages while meeting new friends along the way. What a ride that was!

Awesome doesn't even begin to explain the incredible experience this advanced thinker created for me, you, and the rest of the world to see and explore in our travels; not to mention the timesaving and cost-cutting shortcut that was created for commercial transit and shipping.

I learned that you actually could sail a small ship over a mountain. This concept really grabbed me. It made me realize that so much was possible in this world. So, as an advanced thinker myself, I pondered what the individual who came up with this idea must have gone through. Certainly, there must have been many different ideas about how the feat could be accomplished.

Imagine the logistics of the whole operation, starting with the research on the territories to be involved, which required dealing with the governments of multiple countries, not to mention the engineering and labor it took just to formulate a viable plan for the construction of this remarkable waterway and lock system.

Next, consider the selling he had to do to convince others his advanced thinking could indeed be a real possibility. Hmmm…

Enter yours truly, who wanted very much to take that trip over the mountain in the small ship. This experience was further confirmation for me that no idea was too outlandish, and anything is possible with the right amount of time, effort, patience and perseverance. This realization still empowers me to keep up my own advanced thinking to this day. The future is fertile with positive possibilities.

What can *you* accomplish with advanced thinking?

Maybe you just might cure cancer or discover some new form of energy. I challenge you to pioneer, buck the trend, and do something different. Find a solution to a problem that exists; something that works wonders and creates magic in this world. Do the impossible. Sail over a mountain!

7
Modern Portfolio Theory

Since early in my career, my advanced thinking caused me to want to improve my selling of securities. I soon discovered the "Modern Portfolio Theory." In 1990, three individuals were awarded the Nobel Prize for Economics for their work on the Modern Portfolio Theory. But wait, their research was completed in the early 1950's. Why did it take so long for them to win the prize? At that time, no computer program had the capacity and ability to crunch all the stock numbers to prove the concept worked.

So, it took 40 years to award them the Nobel Prize due to the lack of technology to crunch and process the numbers until the supercomputer was invented. It took even longer for some to catch up and catch on to this technology, and some still haven't yet. These strategies have been around for decades, but they are now going to make more sense and catch on in a more widespread fashion due to this book.

I found a company that had been utilizing this Modern Portfolio Theory concept since 1991. The next year after the prize, as far as my research took me, I found a new success strategy in growing your liquid assets. The more I learned, the greater the pressure became on me to "advance think" about how I could learn and apply this strategy for myself and my clients.

I quickly discovered that I could pay that aforementioned company $2,500 and go to their school to be an advisor while doing business with them. Uh, ha! In 1999, I put my own assets into their asset allocation plan using the true Modern Portfolio Theory. Today, I have over five times the assets.

But there is a hiccup here. In the restatement of the law, third book, a paragraph on page 66 reads, "...the need to change from the "Old Prudent Man Rule" to the "New Prudent Man Rule..." and its rules govern the "Modern Portfolio Theory."

It stated that this was a requirement for the Employee Retirement Income Security Act (ERISA) of 1974, a U.S. federal tax and labor law that establishes minimum standards for pension plans in private industry. ERISA contains rules on the federal income tax effects of transactions associated with employee benefit plans. So, pension plans have been required to use the New Prudent Man Rule since 1974.

Do you wonder why so many big 401k's and 403b's have been sued and lost? I rest my case here. So, why shouldn't this be required of foundations and testamentary trusts to use the new rule as well? Aren't all investments supposed to follow the New Prudent Man Rule? Is it fair to ask why the "good ole boys and girls" and Board members aren't required to follow their fiduciary responsibility, namely, do the best you can for your client? Could this open the case for foundation lawsuits?

I knew about ERISA and the need to change from the Old Prudent Man Rule to the New Prudent Man Rule to stay in compliance with the law. It was now time to turn on my vision thinking. So, I stated my vision for any future investment: the New Prudent Man Rule, and the Nobel Prize for economics 1990 Modern Portfolio Theory would both apply.

Then, one year later, opportunity knocked at the door.

A company was sold, and the foundation donor gave me all of the foundation assets to invest. Now what? I really had to put my advanced thinking cap on, and you would too, if you've never had this happen to you before. Ask yourself, what opportunity or experience have you had like this? None? Well, not many people have, but the opportunity is certainly there.

I asked myself, what kind of portfolio could I put together for this scenario. Answer: none or next to none. But wait, my advanced thinking occasionally gives me some very good ideas. Then, a thought came up. What if I used the asset allocation platform of the new concept here, what would the savings be? Well, immediately, cost savings of all sorts came to light. Uh, ha!

One brilliant idea was to use the Modern Portfolio Theory for this portfolio. Once my research was done, I saw a new way that foundations could use this strategy. Thus, a new approach to foundation investing was born. I had to pursue this new concept and bring it to my clients. So, big changes were about to begin for me and my clients.

8

An Old Plan Needs Revisiting (Non-Qualified Deferred Compensation)

It's about time to revisit an old plan: non-qualified deferred compensation. This concept takes center stage in my first book, "The Deferred Compensation Plan: How to Use Innovative Corporate Strategies to Maximize Your Benefits & Give Your Corporation a Tax Break!", which was published back in 1996. Those same principles not only still hold true today, but they are alive and well for those who are wise enough to employ them.

How many key employees have non-qualified deferred compensation plans? Specifically, plans that you can look at to compare to a government 457 plan. Why not do this for the key employees of a non-profit organization as well?

For starters, COVID 19 caused a large number of small businesses to rely on saved assets to help them to survive. How could they have accomplished that feat? For some, maybe it's too late now, but for the survivors and successful new businesses, it's never too late to learn how to be better prepared. Is a diversified non-qualified deferred compensation plan a reality? Well, let's explore that possibility...

It's very important to state up front that you need a "C" corporation structure in order to do fringe benefits. Why else would you set up a C-Corp? Well, if you make more from your corporation that you plan to spend, why not control what you pay yourself? Is this where your tax problems begin?

Once you have control of what you pay yourself, you can begin to do planning to help your corporation become thrifty, and even plan for yourself and maybe do a bit better than failing or just barely surviving. Doesn't COVID-19 and these resulting challenging times cause you to really want to plan for the times when your business might go through some rough times again in the future? Surely, there are other reasons to become thrifty, but this situation today seems to capture first place. So, where do we go from here?

Transparency is reality. So, first things first, we need to have a **written** plan stating what the corporation is going to do for this particular employee. There has to be an agreement between the corporation before any benefits can be enacted, just to satisfy tax reasons alone. I can't underscore the importance of always having a **written** employee agreement in place. Plus, the corporation should have all of these decisions written and recorded in the corporation minutes and also in the minutes of the annual corporate meeting. When IRS audits take place, this is certainly what they want to see.

Surely the employee would want the agreement in writing for their own protection as well. You may be thinking, what employee? When the corporation hires an employee (any employee), they design a compensation plan for them. This is where non-qualified deferred compensation could come into play. The business owner, CEO, executives, and/or board members often decide who gets selected for the benefit. Now that we have dealt with just a few of the details, can we move on?

Let's set up a non-qualified retirement plan for the owner alone. Maybe the corporation has some cash it can afford to just set aside for savings. Draft an agreement in which the corporation designates savings of X-number of dollars per month. But how can we benefit the corporation and also do something for the owner? Bingo, the corporation saves X-dollars per month and keeps control of the assets. The corporation then decides to invest in an asset allocation fund to grow the assets. It has to be stated in the written agreement that the employee does not own or get this benefit until the specified time in the agreement. The agreement describes when and how the employee gets the assets. Meanwhile, the corporation has ownership of the assets. This lets the corporation use this asset for emergencies, etc., but still remain obligated to fulfill the requirements in the employee agreement. Now, we can see how, if this were reality, many small businesses could use the assets to save the corporation during troubled times.

What else can we do?

Let's say the employee has a disability plan, but, as usual, it doesn't pay enough to cover their needs. What could we do to help with this problem? Ditto, the employee agreement could have a clause stating that, in case of disability, the agreement could also be used to provide additional benefits to the employee, much needed help in their time of need.

Are there other fringe benefits that can be of benefit?

What are the needs for life insurance for the owner and executives? Does he or she have family insurance needs, estate planning needs, etc.? Well, why not have the corporation buy all the life insurance that might be needed, whatever the need. Let the owner or executive **own** the policy. Of course, this is also in the employee agreement. The benefit to the employee is that they get their insurance needs covered by the corporation and only have to include the premium as income and pay tax on the premium.

Next, let's consider how best to payout the retirement benefit to the employee at retirement time. Consider such agreements as 5% of the principal for life, for X-number of years, etc. If the corporation pays the benefits at 5%, and the assets continue to grow at 5%, isn't it likely that the corporation will always still have their assets, which might then be used for various other needs?

Considering the benefits, a corporation's plan for key employees might be the difference between huge success or utter failure. So, this brings about the need for some very important planning, wouldn't you agree?

The Non-Qualified Deferred Compensation Plan Step-by-Step Recap:

Anyone in business should understand corporate deferred compensation. It looks something like this:

Specific benefits are withheld for an employee until he or she retires. At that time, the employee gets the retirement benefit and pays regular income tax on it. And the corporation gets a deduction for the amount of benefit paid to the employee.

Of course, that's the correct definition, but what's innovative about it? Nothing. I'm going to show you something new in the way corporations are using deferred compensation.

The first new wrinkle is likely to amaze you. It's a double whammy, providing up-front benefits and deferred benefits for the corporation and the employee. How can you get it? Let's take a step-by-step walk through the plan and see.

STEP 1: AGREEMENT The corporation enters into a legal agreement to set aside an agreed-on sum of money for the employee. It then sets up an account in the employee's name. The agreement is signed by the executive and the corporation's representative.

STEP 2: THE RESOLUTION The corporation adopts a resolution, promising to carry out the agreement and giving the proper authorities permission to carry out the plans. This is done at the same time the agreement is set up.

STEP 3: THE FUND The corporate officer repositions the agreed-on sum into mutual funds and enters it into the employee's account for proper accounting.

STEP 4: THE MARGIN ACCOUNT Once the money is in the mutual funds, the corporation sets up a margin account. The purpose of this account is to get some additional money to provide life insurance on the employee. Life insurance is a necessary benefit for the employee.

Let's use an example to help show how to get an up-front benefit for both the employee and the corporation:

- Place $30,000 in the employee's account—a conservative margin account will let the corporation borrow 40 percent on the $30,000 equity value; 40 percent of $30,000 is $12,000.
- The $12,000 is put into a life insurance premium. This process is repeated each year

to set aside the deferred compensation for the employee.

- You now have $30,000 plus $12,000 ($42,000) at work for the employee.

STEP 5: OWNERSHIP The employee is given ownership of the life insurance policy. With that done, the employee names the beneficiary and can then control the cash value of the life insurance policy.

A CORPORATE EXAMPLE: ABC company's two key owners set out to accomplish several goals in corporate planning. First, they wish to plan for their own retirement. Second, they want to decide which of their employees receive benefits and pensions. Third, they want to fund a buy-sell agreement in case one of them dies unexpectedly or becomes disabled.

If that sounds complicated, it's not. All they have to do is follow steps one through four, and then agree on the person to be named owner of the life insurance policy, and the person to be the named beneficiary of the policy. Once that is complete, the mutual funds begin growing for their retirement, and the equity in the mutual funds begins paying the premium for the life insurance.

Here's a simple corporate approach: An executive/owner wants to provide key-person protection for the corporation. He would follow steps one through four. Then he'd let the key person have the retirement benefit and allow the corporation to be the owner and beneficiary of the insurance policy.

This deferred compensation plan is as flexible as it is innovative. What's more, the logic is irrefutable. It's completely legal. And it works.

A FAMILY EXAMPLE: Suppose an executive is wealthy and needs liquidity for estate settlement taxes as well as family protection. This executive would probably issue the life insurance policy to his family life insurance trust, just to keep the life insurance out of the estate. The need would be provided for, and there would be no three-year waiting period to get the benefit out of the estate at death.

STEP 6: THE INSURANCE The life insurance policy should be set up to fit the needs of the employee: If a lot of protection is needed, the face amount of the insurance can be set high. However, if the need for coverage is not great, the face amount can be reduced, thus enhancing the growth of the cash value and providing an even greater retirement benefit. Great effort should be made at this point to eliminate any need for personal life insurance outside of this plan.

STEP 7: TAXES When the employee becomes an owner of the life insurance policy, and is given control of it, the amount of the premium payments becomes taxable income to him or her. That's because, in the eyes of the IRS, the premium equates to income since the corporation pays it and the "owner" benefits from it.

After the third year, there should be enough extra cash value or loan value to give the employee access to it to pay the income tax on the insurance policy premium. Later, the employee can borrow against the cash value to provide for family needs, such as their children's education. That money can also be used for early retirement. Since social security doesn't pay until the employee reaches age 62, if the employee retires before age 62, social security won't pay. Thus, the cash value would be extremely important to replace a few years of income.

STEP 8: REPEAT THE PROCESS Employing this concept, you'll repeat the process of repositioning investment money (cash) into mutual funds to make the loan for the second and succeeding years. At the end of each ten-year period, the corporation will sell enough shares to pay off the loans and interest. The corporation gets to deduct the loans and interest and can use growth in the asset to pay for the benefit. This is called changing a liability into a possible profit.

After the loans and interest are paid off every ten years, the remaining mutual funds continue to grow for the employee. Indeed, the funds will continue to grow until the employee's retirement obligation is satisfied by the corporation.

When retirement time comes, the employee becomes the receiver, and several important events go into motion:

- The retiree takes "constructive receipt" of the deferred benefits.
- Having paid off all loans and interest, the corporation puts the remaining mutual funds into a retirement fund account for the employee.
- The corporation starts paying the employee a given percentage of the retirement fund's value. (The percentage was determined and

entered into the minutes when the agreement was drawn up.)

- Those payments continue for the length of time specified in the agreement.

Now the retiree has received the promised deferred benefit, but what about the corporation? Does it benefit? Yes. The corporation gets to deduct the deferred benefit paid to the employee each time a payment is made. What does it cost the corporation to get this deduction? Only the time value of money on the small amount that it has not already received a deduction on. Remember, the corporation also received a deduction on the premium on the life insurance and the interest.

THE HIDDEN BENEFIT TO THE CORPORATION. As a final celebration of the plan's benefits, the employee receives the retirement pay-out, and the corporation gets a substantial tax deduction. That's because the pay-out amount is actually income to the retiree, and a deduction of that size should be a tremendous hidden benefit for the corporation.

Ah, may we live in better, more interesting times.

9

100 Years of Dow Jones History

Let's explore the history of the Dow Jones and its corrections over my lifetime of almost 100 years.

May I begin by asking, has the market been brutal during these years? What can we learn by studying market history? Also, why should we do so over a long lifetime? Could this give us a clue about various investment maximums that we can also study? Let's take the challenge and really break down and look at every year's return. Surely there are more questions, but let's get started.

My being so close to 100 years of age (98), let's look at the dark side of the Dow during these years. Why this first? Our emotions and our behavior may cause us to do things that are not in our best financial interest. Are there some studies out there that prove we know just how bad they are in regard to growing our assets? If you can find them online, look at some of Dalbar's studies in some of the more recent years of his publications.

So, what were the down years and how did they look? There were 31 minus years: approximately one third (1/3) of the last century. Now, let's see if the bad years (correction years) dominate that history. In only 16 of those years, the Dow corrected 10% or greater. There are seven years with real corrections of 20% or greater. Why not add here that those seven years include five of them happening during the Great Depression, from 1920 through 1937. If we take those five years out of the seven years, that should teach us to not do the things that cause them. Enough about corrections, what else happened?

What about what happened in the years where the return was greater than 10%? Could our assets really compound during these years? Does this cause us to think, how could we be in the market all these years, and really just follow this market through our working years and through our retirement years? Can we question that statement when we find that there were 44 years with 10% or greater returns? But let's look at the kicker here. So, 22 of these years the return was 20% or greater, and 32 of the years the return was 15% or greater. Yes. Now looking back over these 44 years, the compounding could have done wonders for us. Then we see that there were 17 of them with returns of 25% or greater. What a revelation! It's hard to stop here, but what else is possibly hidden from us?

What was the Dow close (actual number) beginning in 1920 and at the end of the year in 2020? Can you believe it was **only** 71.95%, down 32.90% in 1920. In my birth year, 1924, it closed at 120.51% up 26.16%, with the ending year we find the Dow close to be 30,606.48, up 7.45%. Can we say, what a ride?

Wait, let's look at the years 1973 and 1974. Who can remember or have read about the gas shortage? Here's some numbers for reference: 1973 close 850.86, down 16.58%, and 1974 close 616.24, down 27.57%. This is mentioned because of our current gas problem today.

Surely, we realize that the Dow will rise and fall daily, as do our attitudes; likely caused by a happening, or what someone said or did that day. Does this make some sense? Just follow the market (and there are some know how to do it), even the small investor can. Can we learn from a famous quote from the financial genius and coach, Sir John Templeton? He said, "If you are a long-term investor, you will view a bear market as an opportunity to make money." This has certainly been true these last 23 years for me. What a miracle it was for me to learn how to do this!

So, where can we go from here?

In the years 1929, 1930, and 1931, we had the only complete meltdown in the last 100 years. Adding these down years: 1929 minus 17.17, 1930 minus 33.77, and 1931 minus 52.67 they total 103.61%, so, here was our meltdown. Wait, the Dow close in 1932 was a positive 59.93%, still a minus, but in 1933, it was a very positive year with the Dow closing with a positive return of 66.69%, closing at 99.90%. Then 1933, 1934, 1935 and 1936 were all positive return years. Enough to make up for the meltdown. Could this lead to discovering if there are circuit breakers in the market? Was there a need for some kind of action to slow rapid decline during daily operation of the Exchange? Let's explore this point...

Exchange

The governing body for securities activities is known as the Security Exchange Commission (SEC). In its wisdom from seeing what happens when major corrections start happening, the SEC started what we know as circuit breakers in daily market trading. This, they must have reasoned, would slow a major downturn. So, there are three of them. A 7% drop will trigger a 15-minute halt in exchange trading. A 13% drop in the market will cause the market to stop again. Then a 20% drop in the market will cause the market to close for the day. Why have circuit breakers? Could this be in an effort to slow the herd mentality? We should appreciate this.

Government Market Involvement, Possibly?

Googling the "Plunge Protection Team" (PPT), you find that this is a team of special cabinet members who advise the President about turbulence in the market. Why?! This is a secret team that meets when fear of a big market correction exists. What does this lead us to find out? This fund was activated March 24, 2020, known as "Exchange Stabilization Fund and Covid 19 CRS reports." This can be used to buy stock index futures, possibly like the S&P 500 or the NASDAQ 100 to scotch the market. So, was this done to help the market correct? I'll leave this thought with you to maybe cause you to appreciate the possibility of having a stable market. Now we might see why the market has been such a great factor in America becoming such a great nation. Where does this lead us?

My Vision—Late 1990's

My vision was how to truly follow a market, truly diversified, and to be able to receive market returns as they happen. What had I learned to cause such mind stimulation? It was certainly learning about "The Nobel Prize for Economics, 1990", and some teams that were truly using the concept. Then opportunity strikes.

Cost Reduction—Foundation's Portfolio

An opportunity came along for me to help a foundation to get funded and begin its first operations. Opportunity gave me the chance to cut out basically all of the major costs of setting up investment portfolios and operating them. **Now, 22 years have passed, and the annual compound return of their grants has been 8.395%.** This is over 3% greater than the required 5%. There have been many more charities helped with the extra 3%. What an experience. So far, can we sum up what we have learned, and can we pass it on?

Stock Certificate Ownership

A company needs more capital to carry out its mission and the decision is made to sell stock ownership in the company. Someone buys shares of the company and receives a certificate of ownership, which they will hold. Now, this certificate is worthless unless someone will purchase it from them. The company has the cash for its use and the owner of the stock hopes the company will prosper and someone will give them a profit on their shares. Now, can we visualize that all of the stocks sold in the US and the world allows these companies to have that money to operate for free? Is that saying or is that saying, the public ownership of all the various companies' stocks, sold in the US, is making all these companies able to continually operate? Now, can you visualize how this helped America become great?!

Knowing These Facts

We could just let this chapter speak for itself, which is exceptionally revealing, but by learning how to own enough stocks and bonds, etc. to "own the market", we can learn how to receive "market returns." We now have two major companies operating funds large enough to help us "own the market," thus earning market returns. We can say this movement has existed long enough to bring a lot of investing together. This is promoting better estate building. **The kicker here is that**

foundations, individuals, companies, states, cities, etc. can all do this. What opportunities!

100 Years of Dow Jones History

The best way to predict the future is to understand the past. That's why I have included the historical data of the Dow in the charts on the pages that follow.

Dow Jones Industrial Average - Historical Annual Data

Year	Average Closing Price	Year Open	Year High	Year Low	Year Close	Annual % Change
2021	33,612.36	30,223.89	35,625.40	29,982.62	35,294.76	15.32%
2020	26,890.67	28,868.80	30,606.48	18,591.93	30,606.48	7.25%
2019	26,379.55	23,346.24	28,645.26	22,686.22	28,538.44	22.34%
2018	25,046.86	24,824.01	26,828.39	21,792.20	23,327.46	-5.63%
2017	21,750.20	19,881.76	24,837.51	19,732.40	24,719.22	25.08%
2016	17,927.11	17,148.94	19,974.62	15,660.18	19,762.60	13.42%
2015	17,587.03	17,832.99	18,312.39	15,666.44	17,425.03	-2.23%
2014	16,777.69	16,441.35	18,053.71	15,372.80	17,823.07	7.52%
2013	15,009.52	13,412.55	16,576.66	13,328.85	16,576.66	26.50%
2012	12,966.44	12,397.38	13,610.15	12,101.46	13,104.14	7.26%
2011	11,957.57	11,670.75	12,810.54	10,655.30	12,217.56	5.53%
2010	10,668.58	10,583.96	11,585.38	9,686.48	11,577.51	11.02%
2009	8,885.65	9,034.69	10,548.51	6,547.05	10,428.05	18.82%
2008	11,244.06	13,043.96	13,058.20	7,552.29	8,776.39	-33.84%
2007	13,178.26	12,474.52	14,164.53	12,050.41	13,264.82	6.43%
2006	11,409.78	10,847.41	12,510.57	10,667.39	12,463.15	16.29%
2005	10,546.66	10,729.43	10,940.55	10,012.36	10,717.50	-0.61%
2004	10,315.51	10,409.85	10,854.54	9,749.99	10,783.01	3.15%
2003	9,006.64	8,607.52	10,453.92	7,524.06	10,453.92	25.32%
2002	9,214.85	10,073.40	10,635.25	7,286.27	8,341.63	-16.76%
2001	10,199.29	10,646.15	11,337.92	8,235.81	10,021.57	-7.10%
2000	10,729.38	11,357.51	11,722.98	9,796.03	10,787.99	-6.17%
1999	10,481.56	9,184.27	11,497.12	9,120.67	11,497.12	25.22%

Dow Jones Industrial Average - Historical Annual Data

Year	Average Closing Price	Year Open	Year High	Year Low	Year Close	Annual % Change
1998	8,630.76	7,965.00	9,374.27	7,539.07	9,181.43	16.10%
1997	7,447.01	6,442.49	8,259.30	6,391.70	7,908.30	22.64%
1996	5,739.63	5,177.45	6,560.91	5,032.94	6,448.27	26.01%
1995	4,494.28	3,838.48	5,216.47	3,832.08	5,117.12	33.45%
1994	3,794.22	3,756.60	3,978.36	3,593.35	3,834.44	2.14%
1993	3,524.92	3,309.20	3,794.33	3,242.00	3,754.09	13.72%
1992	3,284.08	3,172.40	3,413.20	3,136.60	3,301.11	4.17%
1991	2,929.04	2,610.64	3,168.83	2,470.30	3,168.83	20.32%
1990	2,679.45	2,810.15	2,999.75	2,365.10	2,633.66	-4.34%
1989	2,510.33	2,144.64	2,791.41	2,144.64	2,753.20	26.96%
1988	2,061.48	2,015.25	2,183.50	1,879.14	2,168.57	11.85%
1987	2,277.53	1,927.31	2,722.42	1,738.74	1,938.83	2.26%
1986	1,793.10	1,537.73	1,955.57	1,502.29	1,895.95	22.58%
1985	1,327.99	1,198.87	1,553.10	1,184.96	1,546.67	27.66%
1984	1,178.59	1,252.74	1,286.64	1,086.57	1,211.57	-3.74%
1983	1,190.78	1,027.04	1,287.20	1,027.04	1,258.64	20.27%
1982	884.53	882.52	1,070.55	776.92	1,046.54	19.60%
1981	932.95	972.78	1,024.05	824.01	875.00	-9.23%
1980	891.14	824.57	1,000.17	759.13	963.99	14.93%
1979	844.38	811.42	897.61	796.67	838.74	4.19%
1978	821.13	817.74	907.74	742.12	805.01	-3.15%
1977	894.37	999.75	999.75	800.85	831.17	-17.27%
1976	975.20	858.71	1,014.79	858.71	1,004.65	17.86%
1975	802.89	632.04	881.81	632.04	852.41	38.32%
1974	759.13	855.32	891.66	577.60	616.24	-27.57%
1973	924.07	1,031.68	1,051.70	788.31	850.86	-16.58%
1972	950.08	889.30	1,036.27	889.15	1,020.02	14.58%
1971	884.87	830.57	950.82	797.97	890.20	6.11%
1970	753.12	809.20	842.00	631.16	838.92	4.82%
1969	875.72	947.73	968.85	769.93	800.36	-15.19%
1968	903.96	906.84	985.21	825.13	943.75	4.27%
1967	879.48	786.41	943.08	786.41	905.11	15.20%

80

Dow Jones Industrial Average - Historical Annual Data

Year	Average Closing Price	Year Open	Year High	Year Low	Year Close	Annual % Change
1966	872.78	968.54	995.15	744.32	785.69	-18.94%
1965	910.70	869.78	969.26	840.59	969.26	10.88%
1964	834.09	766.08	891.71	766.08	874.13	14.57%
1963	714.69	646.79	767.21	646.79	762.95	17.00%
1962	639.14	724.71	726.01	535.76	652.10	-10.81%
1961	691.74	610.25	734.91	610.25	731.14	18.71%
1960	618.02	679.06	685.47	566.05	615.89	-9.34%
1959	632.57	587.59	679.36	574.46	679.36	16.40%
1958	491.26	439.27	583.65	436.89	583.65	33.96%
1957	476.07	496.03	520.77	419.79	435.69	-12.77%
1956	493.21	485.78	521.05	462.35	499.47	2.27%
1955	442.69	408.89	488.40	388.20	488.40	20.77%
1954	334.34	282.89	404.39	279.87	404.39	43.96%
1953	275.84	292.14	293.79	255.49	280.90	-3.77%
1952	270.35	269.86	292.00	256.35	291.90	8.42%
1951	257.41	239.92	276.37	238.99	269.23	14.37%
1950	216.28	198.89	235.47	196.81	235.41	17.63%
1949	179.67	175.03	200.52	161.60	200.13	12.88%
1948	179.78	181.04	193.16	165.39	177.30	-2.13%
1947	177.48	176.39	186.85	163.21	181.16	2.23%
1946	191.52	191.66	212.50	163.12	177.20	-8.14%
1945	169.66	152.58	195.82	151.35	192.91	26.65%
1944	143.32	135.92	152.53	134.22	152.32	12.09%
1943	134.92	119.93	145.82	119.26	135.89	13.81%
1942	107.15	112.77	119.71	92.92	119.40	7.61%
1941	121.93	130.57	133.59	106.34	110.96	-15.38%
1940	134.64	151.43	152.80	111.84	131.13	-12.72%
1939	142.57	153.64	155.92	121.44	150.24	-2.92%
1938	132.36	120.57	158.41	98.95	154.76	28.06%
1937	166.45	178.52	194.40	113.64	120.85	-32.82%
1936	162.07	144.13	184.90	143.11	179.90	24.82%
1935	120.35	104.51	148.44	96.71	144.13	38.53%

81

Year	Average Closing Price	Year Open	Year High	Year Low	Year Close	Annual % Change
1934	98.16	100.36	110.74	85.51	104.04	4.14%
1933	84.50	59.29	108.67	50.16	99.90	66.69%
1932	64.53	74.62	88.78	41.22	59.93	-23.07%
1931	138.60	169.84	194.36	73.79	77.90	-52.67%
1930	236.04	244.20	294.07	157.51	164.58	-33.77%
1929	313.54	307.01	381.17	198.69	248.48	-17.17%
1928	226.17	203.35	300.00	191.33	300.00	49.48%
1927	176.07	155.16	200.93	152.73	200.70	27.67%
1926	153.00	151.08	166.14	135.20	157.20	4.05%
1925	134.40	121.25	159.39	115.00	151.08	25.37%
1924	99.65	95.65	120.51	88.33	120.51	26.16%
1923	94.87	98.77	105.38	85.91	95.52	-2.70%
1922	93.24	78.91	102.76	78.59	98.17	21.50%
1921	73.39	72.67	81.50	63.90	80.80	12.30%
1920	90.01	107.23	108.85	66.75	71.95	-32.90%
1919	99.79	82.60	119.62	79.35	107.23	30.45%
1918	80.97	76.68	89.07	73.38	82.20	10.51%
1917	87.87	96.15	99.18	65.95	74.38	-21.71%
1916	95.27	98.81	110.15	86.42	95.00	-4.19%
1915	74.45	54.63	99.21	54.22	99.15	81.49%

Dow Jones highs and lows by year

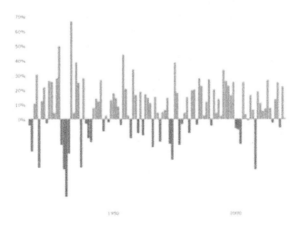

10

Wakeup Calls and Market Corrections

Now that we've discussed the history of the Dow Jones, hopefully you have a better understanding of the cyclic nature of the stock market.

For starters, we should be thankful for market corrections. Here's why...

How many market corrections have there been between 1900 and 2021? How did we treat the ones we knew about? Were there other effects in the general economy that might have been caused by a market selloff? Does the selloff create opportunities for market recovery? How do we take the market selloffs, personally or optimistically? Can we stay humble, or do we let the market do it for us? Should we think, then ask ourselves, where do I stand when I realize that a selloff has happened? Does where I have been sitting in my thinking have any effect on my decision making? Is this where you let your emotions take control of your actions? Is it possible to ask if there are some changes to consider in your thinking and actions that might cause you to pause and ask how can you best find some calculated education that can help solve the problem now and create a path for the future? Where do we go from here?

As Al Frank said, "Without sell off, there are no rallies." So, should we really be thankful for the corrections (selloffs)? If we should, why? Could calculated education give us some answers and maybe motivation to find out what it is and how we, even small investors, can learn it? Then, put it into practice. Well, we have to go back a few years, to 1990. That's when the Nobel Prize for Economics was won by three individuals who had done a lot of calculated study, starting back in the 1950's era. Well, since 1991 there are at least two companies currently following calculated education, in my opinion. So, there are facts and data available to evaluate how this calculated education has worked.

If humans have lived and evolved over billions of years, curiosity might prompt us to ask what the important role that education has played in our progress to date. So, gambling instead of investing is, as Wilson Mizner said, "The sure way of getting nothing for something." So, are we gambling or investing with our assets? "A gambler is a person who doesn't know the marker," Jesse Livermore once said.

Could we now think and understand that we do not have the calculated education to know the market? Should we really realize that we can't do the investing by ourselves? We might find that the more successful investors find an educated investment coach to guide them in their goal. Can we come up with some facts that might comprise calculated education?

If you are gambling, are you at least diversified? If you don't know the market, how could you possibly know how to diversify? Why is it very important to diversify? Don't we have a need to keep our losses as low as possible in the selloff of the market? Will calculated excessive diversification help us possibly keep our losses low in the selloff? If we can accomplish this, it might help us to be in a position to follow the market when it rallies. Being in a position to follow the market in the usual rapid comeback is the key to using calculated excessive diversification. How else is calculated excessive diversification possibly a key to possible success? The Nobel Prize used the principle of owning all of the asset classes of equities. This is how calculated excessive diversification happens. What else did the Nobel Prize accomplish?

Risk might be even a problem for some gamblers, but surely is for most investors. The winners of the prize found that by repositioning the asset in the portfolio they could lower the risk and increase the return. Thus, by changing the percentage of the asset and the kind of asset, the risk changed. Once you have the desired assets in the portfolio to accomplish calculated excessive diversification, you could change the percentage of each asset owned to establish certain amounts of risk. How neat, one can select the amount of risk they are willing to take. So, what problem is left, now that we can own an investment portfolio that owns enough equities to possibly follow the selloff and the rallies. What's next that you need to know and do?

If you own a portfolio now, it's not likely you know what risk you are taking for the return you are receiving. One must analyze your portfolio to find out what risk you are taking, so that would help in one's decision as to the risk to take in a calculated excessively diversified portfolio.

Isn't it time to elaborate on the use of calculated excessive diversification as a solution? It was very interesting to find quotes from Ron Vinder mentioned in the last paragraph of Evie Liu's article, "When (and Why) Bigger is Better", *Barrons*, January 11, 2021. Ron Vinder is an advisor with Morgan Stanley's private wealth management. Two of his quotes are: "Is that by introducing a riskier asset class, such as small caps—the whole portfolio will become more aggressive," and, "the more asset classes a portfolio has, the more conservative it gets." These quotes are very close to what you would find by studying The Nobel Prize for Economics in 1990. So, the asset allocation portfolio uses practically all asset classes in the portfolio and removes or adds some classes to help a client arrive at the risk one is willing to take. With that, we know about calculated excessive diversification.

So, why is all of this incredibly timely and important right now? COVID-19 has created a WORLD MARKET CORRECTION, not a 2000 or 2008 correction. You will learn the difference as time moves on. This correction started February 24, 2020. So, what is happening, and are you prepared for what is still to come?

In my years of experience, 39 as a financial coach, 20 as a current foundation financial advisor, 10 as a big testamentary trust advisor and foundation consultant, my experience has taught me that people basically will not listen or learn really how to be well prepared for events and downturns such as those that are occurring today. So, what do you need to know to correct this problem, you ask?

First, let's discuss why you should be concerned about a huge wake-up call. Can you say that you have studied the cost that comes out of your ETF and mutual funds annually each year? You've got to do this before you can really calculate your return accurately. Cost is made up of management costs, gross expense ratio, probably a 12b1 fee, and your advisor's fee, just to name the obvious ones. Other costs are there, but not as obvious, such as turnover of portfolio cost, and trading cost, etc. Please read the article, "How Independent Brokers Make Money," recently published in *Barron's* publication by Daren Fonda. Then let it blow your mind as to what other fees and costs they charge you. When you do not know your cost, you really have to wonder which class of ETF or mutual fund they sold you.

May I give you an example to wake you up? Go to Morningstar and print out all the classes (I went to the A's) and found American Funds Global Growth Port A through R6. I found 14 of them. I studied the 5-year returns, and the low one was 5.60% and the best one was 7.29%. What caused this wide range of returns? You guessed it, cost.

So, you think you are prepared for a huge wake-up call? Can you answer the question as to which classes you own in all of the asset classes of equities in your ETFs and mutual funds portfolio? As we will discuss more in the next chapter, you really need to have a qualified professional analyze your portfolio and help you study the things you are doing that might keep you from being prepared for any market correction. People have to know why they need to make changes before they will consider them. That is just human nature. Then, they will not correct the problem until you have satisfied them that there is a real solution that is working and has worked, but they did not know about it. Is there another example that I could give to help you grasp what I'm saying?

Another example, if I may, is regarding a recent analysis of a potential client who held $3 million of assets in 18 ETFs and mutual funds. The difference in the three-year return of his 18 funds was 1.47% less than he could have owned in a low-cost asset allocation plan with much less cost structure than his ETFs and mutual funds. Compounding his $3 million another 1.47% for the next 30 years, which he is expected to live, and you will see how much more the allocation using the 1990 Nobel Prize for Economics could do for him. He is definitely not prepared for the wake-up call because, if you are truly diversified, you can usually go up with the rapid growth as the market rises very fast to get back to where it was when it corrected. So, compounding approximately $3 million over 30 years at 1.47% would provide this person with approximately $1,647,836 in 'extra' money. Now can you see how a little extra return over a few years can make a huge difference?

Behavioral research done by "Dalbar 2019 QAIB Report" for the period ending December 31, 2018, shows the S&P 500 lost 4.38% for the year while the average equity investor lost a staggering 9.42% in 2018. Page 14 of the same report shows the following behavior: loss aversion, narrow framing, mental accounting, diversification, anchoring, herding, regret, media response and optimism is what causes major problems for the average investor. Behavior is a major problem for most when it comes to investing.

Do you really want to know if you are prepared for a huge wake-up call? May I help you further determine if you are?

With so many market corrections since January 1, 2000, and may I say some bad ones, how have you fared during these hiccups? Is it time to consider some of the things that are available to maybe improve your return, cool your fear, and just relax and follow the market?

Ask yourself, are you currently trusting someone else to choose investments for you? Now you have to be honest with yourself and answer some questions which will tell you how prepared you are for the next big wake-up call. Has your portfolio kept your return close to the Dow return for the last 11 years, since March 9, 2009? Do you even know the answer to that question? Are you someone who moves in and out of the market? Do you know what risk you are taking for the return you are getting? Do you know all of the different asset classes of mutual funds or ETF funds? Do you know how many equities there might be in a truly diversified portfolio? Do you know how to determine what risk factor (standard deviation) you have in your portfolio and how it relates to a portfolio, like fixed income, balanced or moderate, long-term or aggressive? Do you know how percentage fixed income and equities relate to what risk portfolio you are in? We can go on with this because there are 15-plus things in your portfolio that have an effect on the return you receive.

Should you decide to invest in an investment of any kind, surely you understand there will be risk involved. So, risk exposes us to possible loss in something valued. Many, many people invest in mutual funds, which own stocks. As financial conditions exist in different businesses, their stocks might be subject to less or greater chance of becoming better, or even a total failure. Thus, the risk involved with mutual funds. Morningstar data pages show this risk as a standard deviation. The stocks being held in the fund indicate how much risk is involved with each different kind of mutual fund. So, risk should be a major consideration when one is choosing which funds to own.

When you decide to open an account, five major platforms are available to choose your risk. They are fixed income, balanced or moderate risk, long term growth, or aggressive growth. Percentages in different amounts, like 50% equities and 50% fixed income. This is how risk may be selected. The risk you pick should indicate what return you might expect. While we consider the risk involved in a fund, the cost of owning the fund gets exposed, so let's consider cost.

What a subject to explore in looking at cost in our investments. For starters, some funds are offered with upfront sales charges and can also show up as deferred sales charges. These charges may range between 3.50% to 5.75%. It should be noted that in the case of deferred sales charges, the expense ratio appears, in most cases, to be higher than a fund with no upfront sales charge. Now that we have mentioned the expense ratio of the fund, this is where this stated percent of the fund assets is charged each year before any return might happen. The fund manager charges this fee for the expenses to manage the fund. Many of these funds can have very high fees, and that surely might cause your return to be less than expected. At the same time the expense ratio is found, some funds have 12b1 fees. This extra fee is charged just to give the broker, dealer, and the advisor a little extra fee money. The SEC frowns on this fee. Enter the no-load funds, which promote no upfront sales charges. Well guess what, upon analysis of many of them, you guessed it, they have some very high expense ratios. They work just like the expense ratios in the other mutual funds. Now that we know all of this, how can we be aware and still be able to follow the market? Let's see how that works.

The Nobel Prize for Economics 1990 suggests owning all asset classes of equities. There are some 21 of these classes, like small company stocks, small growth stocks, small value stocks, etc. The way one can own all of them, small amount or large investment, is through an asset allocation plan. The asset allocation plan owns all of the asset classes. This is where excessive diversification happens. Once excessive diversification happens and rebalancing occurs, it is possible that the asset allocation may follow the market. Why is this a possibility? The funds, which are asset classes, own enough equities in each fund to follow the market.

So, if one follows the market and would be satisfied with the market returns, one might be able to cool their fear of losing everything, relax and stop jumping in and out of the market. Let's now look at how to choose the risk to help accomplish risk control.

The five platforms are set up, each with a different risk exposure. Maybe considering the time horizon when one might need a part or all of the assets invested, could be a guide in the selection of risk to be tolerated. Once you accomplish this feat, you should be able to relax more. So, how are the platforms set up to establish the risk for each platform? Using the 21 asset classes as the platforms increase risk, some of the lesser risky asset classes of assets are removed. This is why the higher the risk platform, the smaller number of asset classes are held in the platform. It was shown in the Nobel Prize for Economics 1990 to help one invest and stop gambling with the assets you need to grow.

When you add that each asset class of equities is assigned a certain percent that it holds in the asset allocation, we can see that it is possible to choose the risk we want to take. Another part of this endeavor is that the asset allocation has a low-cost structure. There are two asset allocation plans available. One has much lower cost than the other.

When you think about investing outside of your company retirement plans, ask the question, if you have limited assets available, what is available to truly diversify those assets? Let's face it, even in a 401k or 403b retirement plan, there are not enough asset classes holding enough equities for you to truly diversify your account. Do you know how many you should own to be truly diversified? When you learn this, how can you do it? Again, you need a financial advisor you can honestly trust to help you.

When you are truly diversified, you will own somewhere between 20 to 60 thousand different equities in a pool of assets, namely asset allocation accounts that are following the Nobel Prize for Economics 1990. Second, you will learn that a small amount of assets invested has the same diversification as say, a $100,000,000 account would have. Then, in addition, you might learn that what you have been doing is truly gambling with your assets. I realized this on June 2, 1999, when I decided I did not have enough assets ($340,000) to be able to truly diversify my account. So, I moved to an asset allocation plan following the Nobel Prize for Economics 1990. What else should you learn to help yourself?

Now, look at the choices and see if you can determine the objective of the fund or what asset class it is. In a target 401k plan, ask yourself, why would you want to stop taking risk or drastically reduce it when you are expected to live another 30 to 35 years after retirement age? Did you know that there are two asset allocation programs that are following the 1990 Nobel Prize for Economics, where your small account would have the same diversification as one with millions has? Did you know that one of them has a much lower cost than the other? Did you know you have to have an advisor to help you invest in either of those asset allocation plans?

Let's see if you understand when you own some mutual funds or ETF funds, personally, that it will be almost impossible to rebalance the accounts. Rebalance means that you have a different percentage of your assets in different funds and periodically sell that percent of excess in the fund and buy to bring another up to its proper amount of assets. This is truly selling high and buying low. Where do we go from here?

Next, one of the hardest things to learn is, you should always stay fully invested. Why is that so important? Human nature (our minds and our emotions) tell us to protect when things are wrong and repeat it again when things are right. That translates into selling now and buying late or getting back in the market later, when it looks good. Well, what's wrong with that? Guess what, the market has corrected quickly most times, and if you wait, you'll miss the big upturn. So how can you correct this? Here is the key, and why you should use it.

Most times when the market corrects and the upward movement takes place, getting back to where the market started the correction, it happens with big correction days. So, when you own close to the whole market in an asset allocation plan, you are able to pick up most of the equities on the rise. Most important is, do not miss these days. That is why, at the end of the year, your return will not be what you expected when the market has had a big rise. We could go on with this, but you have enough to know if you need to find help. So, is it time to deal with 'what if'?

What if you have decided you are not going to listen and try to improve, what happens to you in a major correction? The first thing to remember is what amount you started your investment with. Why? You have not lost your nest egg until you lose below that number. Then it is definitely time for you to run. Look, the growth you probably had at the beginning of the correction was a piece of paper until you decided to liquidate part or all of your account. You know it's going to move up and down. Knowing the above, try to control your emotions and seek help! You might be proud of your decision and not become one of so many who get in the market when it is high and exit at the bottom of the correction. Why not consider an alternative to the norm. Again, what's that?

Advisors have to hunt for new clients continually, so be different and find an advisor who is always willing to spend time with you until you get comfortable enough with your new learning experience to change to something that has been working a long time for a lot of people who already made the change. Why should you hunt for the advisor? Look, compare advisors at various brokerage houses and see how much time they are willing to spend with you. Most of the time, they will sell you a fund or an EFT and you will not even know what class. They'll get your money and then let you go.

Always find out what the advisor you choose will charge for their service. Then, it is my prayer that a lot of you will learn from what has happened so far and what will happen before this major world correction ends.

It's your choice, you can decide to grow some more, or you can decide to let corrections whip you into a frenzy. Realize that the stories and gossip that are told are almost always on the bad side of the situation. So, ask yourself how many good stories have you had in your life up to now? How important were those stories to you? Have they meant anything to you? Did they cause you to change for the better or for the worse?

My last question to you is, why aren't your idle assets at work?

I could keep going on and on with helping you determine if you are truly diversified and ready for the next huge wake up call. For those of you that are, please join me and become like myself, just waiting to be fully invested and truly diversified when the market correction is over and the market skyrockets to get back where it was before the correction started. Be like me; that is where I make my money!

The highs and lows are like waves, just as in energy, it comes and goes. Learn to surf and ride the waves. Buy low, sell high. Buy and hold for long term gains.

You only recognize a loss when you sell low. Most importantly, be prepared, and don't panic when a market correction occurs.

11

Why You Can't Invest by Yourself Today

With all of the online investment and trading platforms available today, it's easy to fall into the trap of uncalculated, or improperly calculated, investing. Just because you can, doesn't mean you should!

This is a good time to mention that you may hear some of the same things mentioned more than once as we move forward through the remainder of this book. Forgive my repetition, but, if I do repeat something more than once, it's probably important for you to remember. Repetition leads to memorization, recognition, and learning. Have you ever seen the same commercial on TV more than once? Additionally, I'm also trying to prove the point that the same strategies are applicable in multiple scenarios. So, with that being said, let's continue...

One thing that a lot of people have told me over the years is they know nothing about investing. Many have told me about a good investment they made, but how they sold it too soon, or didn't sell it soon enough. If they're honest, they may even disclose how it went from good to bad to worse. Then, they may find a broker to help. Soon, they are buying and selling stocks, but admit they are getting nowhere.

Can we all agree that we were taught nothing about **money and investing** in any of our **schooling**? Doesn't this cause you to want to find some answers to a lifetime investment problem?

For starters, I would like to quote Ashby Daniels in the March 2021 *AARP Bulletin,* a paragraph in the article *Profitable Reading, Advice Drawn from Recent and Forthcoming Books About Money*, *Keep Your Investments Simple*: "I believe being willing to stick to a **diversified portfolio** of **index funds** is the closest thing to an **investing superpower** that exists, in the age of shiny object syndrome. Patience seems to be a much simpler and more satisfying road to our financial goals than always trying to find the next best thing."

So, what are some decisions you've had to make based on your experiences, and do they amplify the need for simplification know-how?

Hopefully, a majority of employees in today's workforce are offered 401k's, 403b's or retirement plans of some kind. In these plans, usually mutual funds are given for the employee to make a choice for their portfolio. If they know nothing about investing, how can they know what to choose for their portfolio? How can they do a good job of diversifying their portfolio? Is this the only concern one might have?

What about choosing their risk tolerance? Is this of equal importance in the selection process? How can one accomplish just these two important decisions? The answer is that most simply can't. There is not enough information offered, in my opinion, for the employee to make an educated and wise decision. Is there a solution to this problem?

How long have there been some answers to calculated diversification, calculated risk selection, and a way to simplify your investment life? Is there experience available to back this up? The answer is yes. I have over 20 years of experience in doing just that. What are some of the simplifications that are solved for the employee and also for their personal investments?

First, go study The Nobel Prize for Economics in 1990. I can't reiterate this enough! This is where it all began, a long time ago. Let's use the following example of how a small family foundation used the things learned in the Nobel Prize over the last 20 years. Note the simplification.

- The foundation found an asset allocation.
- Did not have to put a portfolio together.
- No investment committee was needed.
- Asset allocation had calculated excessive diversification and calculated risk selection.
- No stock or bond study was needed.
- The board of director's portfolio fiduciary responsibility was transferred to the asset allocation money manager.
- No portfolio monitor was needed.
- Asset allocation used the Nobel Prize efficient frontier, enabling the foundation to select the risk they were willing to take, which was a calculated, standard risk.
- Today, there are at least two such asset allocation plans, one with possible lower cost than the other available.
- The portfolio manager makes any changes to the portfolio that are needed.
- The portfolio manager periodically rebalances the portfolio to keep the risk selection in balance.

- Could this possibly eliminate one's emotions in their investment experience?
- The first calculated excessive diversification and calculated risk selection allocation plan was started in the very early 1990's.

So, where do we go from here?

On June 28, 2015, *Investment News* published a viewpoint article, "The Mutual Fund Market Place is broken. Time to fix it." What a wonderful, timely, article! It was an excellent article, but it only scratches the surface of the problem.

For starters, print out a Morningstar page on several different fund companies' growth funds, large or small, US fund and international fund. Then take the challenge to find the nineteen things, one each, on these pages that affect the return on that fund.

Next, print out all the same funds followed on Morningstar pages, on all of the same fund pages of a particular fund company, let's say Vanguard (as mentioned in the aforementioned *Investment News* article). See if you can find over 80 of these. Many of these funds have been stopped and restarted since 2007. Note, that you may find the same stocks in the old fund that are now in the new fund. Is it fair to ask, why stop a fund and start it over? Can you see what the fund return was in any of the previous years, especially the years that had market corrections activity in them? If the fund had some very bad loss years prior to starting it over, an investor might not realize the real risk of the fund. Even with all the above information, the investor would have to see and study the Morningstar data to pick this up.

There's much talk and sales promotion deals that tout beating benchmarks. It's easy to check what a fund has returned over the last ten years on a growth of $10,000.00, versus its benchmark. Morningstar shows this information, and when you run all the funds offered by a fund company, then count the funds that did not beat their benchmark, you might be surprised at the findings.

Of particular interest to a new investor, could be the number of different sales options to purchase in each different fund. As mentioned in the viewpoint article, that number being one, or even up to six, as was found in the Vanguard funds. Even more interesting was the minimums required to open the account in each option. Look at these minimums: $3,000.00, $10,000.00, $100,000.00, $5 million, $100 million, $200 million, and two options had zero minimums to open the accounts.

In further studying sales options to purchase a fund, you should notice and compare the combined expense ratios (as they are reduced when minimums are increased). This should cause you to ask, is diversification of the assets important, and will the return and risk justify taking such a chance on less diversification? Looking at some very large accounts, like foundations, large pension funds, etc. and seeing the amount of assets, like $50 million or $100 million in one mutual fund, you have to wonder why such little attention is paid to risk. The Nobel Prize for Economics in 1990 was a good teacher in this regard.

Curiosity about the practice of fund companies adding one to five bonds in a stock fund or adding one to five stocks in a bond fund, should cause concern. Again, looking at all the Morningstar pages on a particular fund company and studying the holdings report information, you can easily spot this practice. It really should cause concern when you could find 20% or more of the funds were offered this way. Can we ask what the purpose for adding these in the fund is? Could it be to nudge the return up a little? Why would a fund company do this in a large percentage of the funds it offers?

Objectives of the funds will tell us which asset class of investment we want to own. So, we should look at how many of the options to purchase a fund are available in each asset class. Now, see if all 21 asset classes of equities are offered by the fund company. Why? We need to own them all to be very well diversified.

Doing a further study of the holdings report on Morningstar's data page, we can find out how many stocks are held in each fund. Could this really be important? Let's look at someone who is starting to invest in a new fund. We might find that we might lose up to 40% or more or make up to 40% or more in return in our first year. So, the difference in a zero loss and a 40% loss establishes the risk we take at the beginning. Repeating this process over a number of years, say 10, 15, maybe 20 years, as we have grown our asset, having accumulated a large compound return, we find that after a few years that risk has greatly diminished. Thus, we are saying we would have to give up a lot of our growth before we could lose any of our principal.

What about turnover in the fund? Fund companies usually do not talk about the hidden cost of investing in mutual funds. This becomes very important when turnover becomes high. To grasp a look at this, think about the difference in the buy and sell price of one share of stock. When the company sells 100% of the stocks in your fund you own, ask how many shares were in all 100% of the stocks.

Look at the number of shares held in each stock (maybe millions), then take a 100% turnover and you will have a huge hidden drag on your return. But... that is not the end of it. The company has to buy 100% to replenish the portfolio of stocks. I believe that few investors understand that this goes on in active manager investing (picking and selling stocks).

Have you heard about buying low and selling high? (Of course you have, we discussed it in the previous chapter.) How can the individual purchasing one or a few mutual funds accomplish this? The answer is, it usually never happens. One would have to discipline oneself to rebalance each fund individually when the market was high, sell the excess over a percentage they had established, take the sale assets and buy more of the funds they own that had not produced excess return. This just doesn't happen.

Where individual investors really get hurt is when they are sold (B) or (C) class shares. We find that in some (B) class shares, the expense ratio is much higher than the sales load (A) class. The (B) class shares have added a large 12(b)1 fee to the fund cost. In addition, class (B) shares probably have a 5% deferred sales load, should the investor sell before a certain number of years. Let's say the investor holds the fund past the time they would have to pay the deferred sales load to sell. Now let's ask the question, does the investor get relieved of the excess expense ratio and the 12(b)1 extra fee added on when they chose to invest in class (B) shares? You guessed it, they have it as long as they hold the fund. Repeat this for class (C) shares and you see another drag on your return.

Let's enter the investor coach and help the client become a successful investor by following the passive investing method, using the Modern Portfolio Theory, Nobel Prize for Economics in 1990, which now has a 25-year history of getting market rates of return every year.

Asset Allocation Platforms, owning all asset classes of equities in structured index funds (structured to get market rates of return) will help stop the "nonsense" going on in the marketplace.

The bottom line is that you should have your portfolio analyzed so you know what its pitfalls might be. Just moving to another plan without knowing its problems might not help you make a better decision. Find an investment coach experienced in using the Nobel Prize asset allocation plan.

Here are some final thoughts to close this chapter:

- A storm can't wipe out the fleet if the fleet is spread out in different areas (diversified).
- Invest large enough and long enough in an asset allocation fund to see if it works for you.
- Don't change anything for a minimum number of years in order to follow the market.

May you find true investment simplification!

12

Retirement and Asset Accumulation

According to a Gallup poll study, eight out of ten retirees have enough assets to live comfortably in retirement; two out of ten do not. May we flip a coin and ask one of the two who didn't have enough money to live comfortably in retirement, if it's possible for someone to quit their job supervising 21 people at the age of 57 to work for themselves? Yes, that's me. I used to be one of the 20% of people approaching retirement who had not been able to accumulate enough assets to live comfortably in retirement. However, I made some major changes and did something about that late in life. So, now I am actually qualified to write about pre-retirement asset accumulation!

I'd like to reference Mr. John Sullivan's article, which appeared in the second issue of 2020's *401k Specialist Magazine.* It stimulated my advanced thinking to ask, what other crisis could there be for hopeful retirees? In my recent analysis of some target date 401k retirement plans that are followed by Barron's mutual fund listings weekly (my choice of this group was because they are listed in the top 2,500 mutual funds by assets weekly), some very interesting questions came to mind. Could some of these questions indicate that there may be a crisis not only in retiree asset accumulation, but also in target date plans? May we explore this possibility with some very specific questions?

In the last twenty years before retirement age, the age group who retired between the years 2005 through 2020, drastically reduced their risk, compared to the younger age group. Why so? Isn't this the crucial time for this group to ramp up their accumulations? Many may have been raising their children on their own at the time. Could this really be when they complete the process? Now that they are ready to retire, or already have, let's ponder how long they are expected to live. Are they going to live to an average age of 85 or 90? Won't there be a need to keep their assets working to avoid running out of money before they die? Doesn't this create the need to keep some level of risk, so their money continues working for them in order to continue living comfortably in retirement?

In their last twenty years before retirement, why are the returns of this age group in the last five years practically all the same? They are really hardly any different from the younger group who won't retire until 2045 through 2060; however, based on the length of time they have had to amass wealth and capitalize on compound interest, shouldn't their returns be much more impressive? Could this cause a shortage in their accumulation of assets?

Why does, say one age group in one particular company have 10% to 20% in stocks, and another company's employees have 40% in stocks for the same age group? How can this be eliminated? Knowing that risk is reduced from the youngest age group to retirement, why is there only a .03 basis points difference in the standard deviation (risk) between age group 2045 through age group 2060? In the same company, over the last five years of average return, there is only .47 basis points difference in the average returns. Why is this?

Could it be that high turnover in the plans studied might be an indication that active management or stock picking might be happening in an asset allocation plan? Looking at the age group retiring in 2045 through 2060, why, in those years (over 20), would the return, risk, expense ratio, holdings, and turnover be almost the same numbers for each age group? This is hard to understand. Why, in some companies, are 12b1 fees added? When a company has a 1.00% deferred sales load, and they raise the expense ratio drastically, and the funds are held long enough for the deferred sales load to be over, does this extraordinarily high expense ratio and 12b1 fee reduce? Can you see the difference in the 5.00%-plus up-front sales load and the 1.00% deferred sales load? Does the same number of holdings basically through all age groups cause the difference in the 5-year average return to be nearly the same for all age groups? Could all of the above (and there are more questions) cause one to realize there is a crisis? May I ask, is there a solution? What's your opinion after studying the above analysis questions? So, what's a solution?

Why do you need a solution?

For starters, I quit my job at age 57, on August 31, 1981. Back then, you could buy a home for $78,000, a NEW car for $7,000, have a child go to Harvard College for $6,000 or rent a place to live for $315 per month in the best neighborhood. Food was priced affordably as well. So, what's the problem? Just look at the current price of $3.50 to $5.00 for gasoline in the United States, or what a really nice home cost today. It has not only changed the cost of living, but it also changed the amount of your accumulation needs, hasn't it?

So, what's a solution?

This is where I have to get personal. My accumulation started in a big way on June 2, 1999, when I rounded up my assets in the amount of $340,000-plus and invested them in an asset allocation plan that was started in 1991, the very next year after the Nobel Prize for Economics in 1990. Why this one? The research that won the prize for three individuals indicated the need to own all classes of equities and reposition your portfolio to reduce risk, thus increasing return. Along with the "Efficient Market Frontier," this helped you to be able to see what risk you were taking for the return you were receiving.

Did it work for me? You bet. Why? My account had grown to $1,213,159 by July 12, 2019. Plus, my withdrawals had totaled $136,593, which means my total over 20 years was $1,349,752. This happened between June 2, 1999, and July 12, 2019. During that 20-year span, I endured the 2000 correction and the 2008-2009 corrections, along with smaller corrections as well.

Now let's explain the details of the asset allocation. I owned 21 distinctly different asset classes of equities, which had fixed percentages of each asset class and over 17,000 equity holdings in over 40 countries of the world. Quarterly, the account sold any percent in excess in any equity and used the assets to purchase and rebalance any asset class that needed to be brought back to its required percentage. This was selling high and buying low at its best. The portfolio was truly diversified as much as possible. Diversification was the key that made it work.

Note: the only choice one has to make in acquiring these plans is the risk they want to take. Changes can be made in risk as long as your assets are in a qualified account. I will have even better news for you about changing later. What, are there other such plans?

What about more than one such plan?

Yes, there is another such plan with some different improvements; namely, the cost in the different plans is considerably much less than the one I started with. You already know that if you can cut costs and keep all other components the same, it increases your chance for a much better return. This second plan has 70,000-plus holdings in 19 specific asset classes. Like the first plan, the participant only has to pick what risk they want to take and can change as many times as the company allows.

Now, for the part that I promised I would reveal later... The participant can have a personal account in the same kind of asset allocation. So, what's good about that? Both are in ETFs with low cost and the company has a PATENT to help you keep from having capital gains each year, thus saving you personal taxes on your personal investments.

How can you get one of these plans? Well, you can't do them by yourself. These companies only work through advisors like me. Someone has to take you there. That is better for you anyway, because you need a coach to help you, especially in today's post-COVID market.

May we finally achieve retirement asset accumulation where the employee and the sponsor do not have to let someone else make all of the decisions for them! Let's eliminate all of the crisis. Google The Nobel Prize for Economics in 1990 and study everything you can find, write down your questions, then call me and I will explain the prize to you.

13
Fiduciary Responsibility

To help you understand the importance of choosing wisely when it comes to selecting a financial advisor, let's shift gears for a moment and discuss fiduciary responsibility. According to Wikipedia, a fiduciary is: "a person who holds a legal or ethical relationship of trust with one or more other parties (person or group of persons). Typically, a fiduciary prudently takes care of money or other assets for another person. One party, for example, a corporate trust company or the trust department of a bank, acts in a fiduciary capacity to another party, who, for example, has entrusted funds to the fiduciary for safekeeping or investment. Likewise, financial advisors, financial planners, and asset managers, including managers of pension plans, endowments, and other tax-exempt assets, are considered fiduciaries under applicable statutes and laws. In a fiduciary relationship, one person, in a position of vulnerability, justifiably vests confidence, good faith, reliance, and trust in another whose aid, advice, or protection is sought in some matter. In such a relation, good conscience requires the fiduciary to act at all times for the sole benefit and interest of the one who trusts."

Furthermore, Wikipedia adds: "A fiduciary duty is the highest standard of care in equity or law. A fiduciary is expected to be extremely loyal to the person to whom he owes the duty (the "principal") such that there must be no conflict of duty between fiduciary and principal, and the fiduciary must not profit from their position as a fiduciary (unless the principal consents)."

This sounds familiar, right? It should. Since we have dealt with the New Prudent Man Rule, let's explore an example to show if the rule is important in regard to fiduciary responsibility and let's see if it has been tested to establish its true meaning. I think you'll agree the answer should be a resounding yes!

The strict application of the importance of the New Prudent Man Rule is evident in the Alabama court case of First Alabama Bank vs Spragins. First Alabama Bank served as trustee under the will of the former president and chairman of the board of the bank. The stock of First Alabama Bank represented 70% of the total estate of the deceased president. The will specifically relieved the trustee from the duty to diversify. The family agreed to hold the stock. Over the period of administration, stocks, in general, increased in value, but the bank stock did not appreciate to the degree that the overall equity markets did. The family sued the trustee, alleging that the bank had violated its duty by failing to diversify the stock. In spite of the language in the will, the **court held that the beneficiaries suffered a loss**, and ruled that **the executor was liable** and assessed damages based on a return that could have been achieved if the assets were invested in the general securities markets. While the court agreed that the trust document governed the duties and obligations of the trustee, it did not agree that the trust language could be applied here to lessen the duty imposed by the "Prudent Person Standard", aka the New Prudent Man Rule.

Ah ha! Now, we have case law established to possibly help with the new rule requirements.

So, the fiduciary is judged on their decision making rather than after-the-fact analysis of performance. The focus is on the total portfolio assets. The emphasis placed on production of income and preservation of principle is replaced by measurement of total return of the portfolio.

Therefore, we can emphatically say that fiduciary responsibility is of utmost importance.

In regard to your personal assets, you probably wouldn't let an unqualified or under qualified stranger babysit your kids, so why do it with your money? Choose your advisor wisely. Trust someone who practices what they preach and has personal results to back up their strategies. I would never invest your money in a way that I wouldn't do with my own.

It's much more personal, yet somewhat simpler when you're dealing with your own finances; however, when we're talking about foundations and nonprofits, there are usually many more people involved in the decision-making process. Could fiduciary responsibility and, thus, liability reach the governing officers of a foundation and other entities? Well, many states have adopted "UPIA," the uniform prudent investor act. This alone is enough to let us know that the New Prudent Man Rule and ERISA law of 1974 and its 1979 rules are alive and well, and very important.

Here are some thoughts and questions to ponder in regard to investment roles and fiduciary responsibilities:

Who handles the investments of the organization and are they truly qualified to do this? Is there an investment committee, and do they rely on board approval and oversight? How was the portfolio established? Was it done in-house or did the foundation hire a professional? Who in the organization is qualified to monitor the portfolio? Who is qualified in-house to manage the portfolio or did the organization hire a professional to do so? How is total portfolio diversification assured? When and how is rebalancing done? What pressure does all of this contribute to the board of directors, and are they qualified and capable of handling it?

If I were a new board member who was taking on fiduciary responsibility, I would first want to know how the investments were doing when I joined the organization. Here's a quick check-up I do when I am performing some foundation consulting. Look at the 990 return and find the difference in the beginning assets and the ending assets. Divide the beginning assets into the difference. This will give you a return number for last year's 990 return. Next, subtract any gifts, grants, or fundraising that happened that year from the difference between the beginning assets and the ending assets. Now divide the beginning assets into this true difference. This will give you a picture of what happened that year. Then repeat this process for the last 15 years of 990s. There might be some surprises revealed!

Let's revisit the Modern Portfolio Theory for a moment. When a portfolio consists of an asset allocation fund that's holding 19 or more indexed asset classes, just look at what all is eliminated. First off, and maybe most importantly, the fiduciary responsibility is transferred to the investment money manager of the asset allocation portfolio. No monitoring of the portfolio is required of the officers of the foundation or nonprofit. They are also relieved of adding or removing a stock or bond from the portfolio. There's no need to hire someone else to monitor the portfolio; therefore, fewer people are needed to run the foundation, thus reducing administrative expenses. This also frees up time for the CEO and other officers to evaluate grant requests and follow up to be sure their grants are working as planned, etc. Sound intriguing?

We have yet to even discuss the savings, which we will do in the next chapter.

If the Modern Portfolio Theory were to be applied to foundations and nonprofits, let's ask the following question. If all 501(c)3s changed their portfolio operation and adopted the "theory" and established their portfolios in that manner, wouldn't the governing officers' fiduciary responsibility and liability be significantly reduced due to the portfolio diversification alone? Not to mention, can we imagine how much cost savings would also occur with this simple shift? Then can we extrapolate the same transformation to all of the thousands of 501(c)3s in the USA and apply the same cost savings across the board? Just think, this one shift could not only lessen the burden of liability on nonprofits and their officers, but it could produce trillions of dollars of more income within these organizations; income that could be distributed in the form of more, larger grants.

By all means, this is certainly not all of the benefits available to, or the changes needed by foundations and nonprofits. I can give you more. Stay with me...

14

Foundations and Nonprofits

I'd like to now transition into focusing more on foundations and nonprofits; the reason being, years ago, my advanced thinking led me to understand that I could make the best use of my time by helping organizations that helped others, rather than just focusing on one person at a time. I knew that if I could help a foundation improve their operations and increase their returns, then they would have more money to give to other organizations and charities that were doing many good things for a lot of people. With essentially the same amount of time and effort, I could impart some valuable wisdom and advice on individuals and organizations who are dedicated to improving the lives of others and the communities they live in. Look no further than the following example as proof and testament to the validity of my thinking.

Spotlight on an Awesome Foundation:

How do you enhance the quality of life and health in two cities and their surrounding areas? Maybe we could study and emulate an awesome CEO and the amazing board of directors of one particular foundation. Their staff's efforts might give us a clue.

First, realize there are over 1,000 foundations in these two cities alone, plus over 20,000 nonprofits in this particular state. These organizations have put a lot of money to work to help many people rise to a higher level and attain a much better life. Two of these entities have over one billion of combined assets.

Let's also give credit to the state leaders for their efforts to create an environment for these foundations and nonprofits to accomplish their many varied goals. If you look at the two impact studies done by an amazing Alliance of Nonprofits in the last ten years, you'll quickly learn what they have added to the quality of life, health, and the standard of living of their community. Just study the reports and let them wake you up and leave you in awe.

I'd like to single out one of these foundations and place them under the spotlight. Then I'd like to imagine the positive impact that could be possible if we multiplied their efforts by spreading their example to the other 1,000 foundations and 20,000 nonprofits. Let's ask the question, what would these two cities and the state look like without this massive effort and all of the volunteers giving so much of their resources and valuable time to make a difference? You guessed it.

This foundation was created in 1979, a long time ago. So, can we just imagine how many people they have made a difference for in that number of years. Well, that is not all of the story. Another foundation has since been added. Now we can really see the impact and difference they have made for the homeless children and very low-income families. Just one example of one difference made in the small foundation operation. This organization delivers to schools and distributes clothes, shoes, backpacks and so many other things. Ah! Just one vehicle wasn't enough, so now there are plans to add more vehicles, more schools and more supplies.

Let's look at the four major areas where these two foundations concentrate the grants they are able to give each year. How can they expand and improve on the four major focuses that follow: improving community health, expanding the state's health workforce, strengthening the community, and increasing access to health care? It's an admirable initiative and focus that requires a large number of grants to accomplish this. The size of these grants range from $1,000 to $1 million and exceeds over 100 in quantity every year. Now that is truly making a difference.

Much efficiency has to be accomplished in order to make all of this happen. So, the leadership by the CEO and a wide-awake staff are constantly thinking and working outside of the box to make this a priority. They work in the comfort of two office complexes. These facilities also offer a wonderful home for offices for other nonprofits as well.

With all of this happening, we must explore some examples of how a grant could make such a difference in one or more of these focused areas.

In 2012, a wonderful mother endured a three-year battle with leukemia in her 3-year-old daughter, who then spent another nine months fighting a cancerous brain tumor. It takes the kind of courage that maybe only a loving mother could cope with. This particular mother founded a nonprofit. It is one of the many nonprofits that are established to make a big difference happen for the less fortunate. Again, with over 20,000 nonprofits in the state, the citizens have the privilege of knowing their less fortunate neighbors can find help.

Another example of a wonderful CEO, with more than one CEO position, has returned to lead a nonprofit organization that has been helping children and families for nearly 60 years. This CEO took their clothing distribution program to a new level when she created the aforementioned foundation and doubled the number of children who are served each year. She states that the foundation grants make it possible to make a great difference.

One more example is how one foundation scholarship to a community college has helped in improving the hospital workforce. One of their scholarships went to an individual EMT firefighter who was having trouble making enough money to support his family. The recipient was granted the scholarship twice, and he graduated with a 4.0 GPA in radiology. He is now employed at a hospital, which was part of the birth and founding of the same foundation.

So, what can be done to help increase these major grants from the 1,000 foundations and over 20,000 nonprofits in the state? There is a way! Since the

Nobel Prize for Economics in 1990, two companies have been steadily increasing the returns on their assets by using the academic research and investment strategy to cut much of the costs associated with the foundation and nonprofit operations. One of the companies that was started in 1991 now has a 28-year track record with above average returns and impressive cost-cutting and expense reduction.

Using the same Nobel Prize winning research, a foundation in another state, since May of 2000, has been able to give grants amounting to 150% of the original corpus, and still has 120% of its corpus left. Most impressively, they never had to do a fundraiser. Cost savings and good returns have made this possible.

Past performance does not guarantee future results. The Dow Jones correction on March 9, 2009, ended with an average of 6,547. On Friday, August 30, 2019, the Dow Jones average closed at 26,362.25. This was 19,000-plus points higher than the end of the 2008 correction. **So, can we ask how our personal portfolios, foundations and nonprofits have responded in such a great bull**

market? Personally, I have gained over four times the assets I put to work since June 2, 1999.

During the last two years alone, a second company drastically cut their costs in the invested assets for the foundations and nonprofits, as much as ½ of a percent. So, as a result, in the last five years, this company has produced a return over 1.25% greater than the other company. This particular company now has over $23 billion in foundation assets at work.

I know this to be true because I have been the financial advisor for the aforementioned **out-of-state** foundation since May 2000. Now I want to share my experience with other foundations and nonprofits in hopes of helping them increase their returns and, subsequently, be able to do more good deeds for more people in their communities.

Let's focus on what we can become. It's time to grow some more. Maybe we can all change for the better. Teamwork makes the dream work!

15

A Model for Foundation Transformation

This is a MUST-READ for any executive, CEO, or board member who is interested in helping effect positive change. Anyone with a 401k or 403b fund may want to pay attention as well.

The focus of this chapter is to convey the very simple principle that, for every dollar in cost reduced, your return will increase. A quote comes to mind: "It's not what you make that matters, it's what you keep that counts."

The National Association of Nonprofit Organizations & Executives (NANOE) website (www.nanoe.org) states the following: "Charity is in desperate need of an overhaul. Current legislation, tax laws, industry standards, outdated philosophies, organizational structures and practices stop the sector from growth on all fronts. Yet, for the past 20 years, government and philanthropic communities have relied more and more on the nonprofit sector to tackle many social and environmental issues. Simply put, industry standards have not kept up with or changed to meet the new demands of the 21st century."

I recently connected with the president of NANOE and had a few very constructive conversations with him. He is working toward the same goals that I am, just on the administrative side of the table. I drafted a letter to him as follows:

Dear Mr. Fawcette,

After finding NANOE and reading the three sentences on your website, I became excited to learn that someone else is working to help nonprofit organizations besides myself. This information tells me that we have a lot in common and that we should explore the possibility of working together to help achieve the transformation of nonprofits. It was a pleasure speaking with you yesterday. May we explore helping each other by working together?...

This book, particularly this chapter, will be instrumental in my quest to help create, improve, and increase positive changes through the efforts of foundations and nonprofits.

Modern Foundations and the Benefits They Provide

It seems that the earliest legislation that introduced the first explicit definition of a private foundation was in 1894, at least that's the earliest date I could find.

We already know that foundations have been doing a great job of awarding grants over the years. Having been a foundation consultant and financial coach for some 20-plus years, may I ask the question, based on my experience and large amounts of assets I manage that provide grants, is it time for assets to provide more grants, and is it time for a review of the foundations to see what improvements can be made in their operations?

I can give you a good example of some consulting I did for a foundation with well over $100 million in assets. I found there to be over $50 million invested in only eight mutual funds. One of these eight funds had 13 fund classes. The quarterly report of the foundation did not indicate which fund class was sold to them. Why is that a problem? If we look at the five-year return and the gross expense ratio, you will find a wide range between the lowest return and the highest return of the 13 fund classes. Therefore, you would also find a wide range between the lowest gross expense ratios and the highest ones.

Further investigation reveals illiquid investments along with some tax shelter types. Could you question the diversification in this portfolio? Also, could you question the cost to structure this by the broker dealer? There were some other problems that will not be mentioned here. After the problems were discussed with the CEO, he stated that he cannot move the portfolio. To me, this raises the question of why? It's obvious there were no improvements made after our meeting.

Let's now move on to foundation grants.

May we agree that the most important functions of each of these organizations is their portfolios and their creation, along with their continued operation? If set up properly, as well as operated properly, most of the time there are no problems with foundations. Just think, is it possible to not have to put a portfolio together, ever, beginning with its creation and throughout its continued operation? The answer is an astounding yes! Is there history of this being done, and was there a basis for doing this before it got started? Yes, and yes! What is the length of the history of this having been done? The answer is 22 years. Were there market corrections during this 22-year period that could challenge these 22 years of operation? Certainly, some of the worst market corrections happened, and they were the bad, bad ones. So, what is so special about not having to put a portfolio together?

Fees and Costs—How Many and How Much?

First, let's question what fees the foundations are paying and to whom. What is the cost associated with putting a portfolio together? Who puts the portfolio together, and do they charge a fee? Is the investment committee, if there is one, paid a fee? Do they have a portfolio of mutual funds and then hire a broker to buy and sell stocks and bonds daily? If so, what is this investment, and how is this person paid: salary or salary plus commissions? If the portfolio is to be stock picking and bond purchasing, and maybe purchasing some mutual funds, what is the cost of the people who do these things and continue to do them forever? If there isn't an investment committee, is there an investment representative member in the group? If so, what are their fees? Who monitors the portfolio and decides to implement the changes needed? What is this cost? How is diversification handled or is there no responsibility? What is the risk of portfolio performance? How is risk determined, and who is responsible for choosing the risk? What is the standard deviation of the portfolio, and what is that number? What is the cost of the trading done in changing the portfolio mix, and also the cost of replacing the mix?

What other fees are foundations paying?

What about the fees in the mutual funds? In most, there are at least five or more fund classes in each fund. So, can we ask if they even know which class was sold to them? Are the fees the same in each different fund class? The answer is no. Is there a security rule that requires the financial advisor to do the best he can for the client? The answer is yes. So, should the advisor sell the client the best one of the fund classes? You know this to be true for sure!

Now comes turnover in the portfolio. What is that cost and is there realization that this cost is a hidden one? Look at the difference in the buy and sell price of an equity. Could this be close to .50 cents per share? Now, look at how many million shares are in a mutual fund. Isn't this huge expense hidden to the investor?

Realize that even in no-load mutual funds, there are expense ratios, management fees and 12b1 fees in some funds. Note that there are usually 10 or more fund classes in mutual funds. Most of the time, which one is sold to you is probably not revealed to you. Why do you need to know this? The classes have different expense ratio costs, management fees, and whether or not there are 12b1 fees. Even look at index funds, what cost exists here? Is there a major reason to do this? You bet!

As we look at each fund class operation for the extended time, we will find that the return is different for each class, because it will have a different return. To see the big difference, look at the last five and ten years of the fund return. Then you will see how important this is! Ask yourself, is there a difference in the risk of each fund class? Even the SEC, when auditing, might look to see if you purchased the lowest cost fund class and whether or not there is a 12b1 fee in your fund. I could go on with this, so let's just move on to some other major costs.

Next, let's talk about a board to advise these organizations. Are they paid fees, and are they covered in any pension fund, the same as employees? What about the training cost to train new board members? Is there a transportation cost to get board members to meetings? I certainly question this. What about fiduciary responsibility? Is insurance purchased for protection, and isn't this an annual expense? Does the CEO know the cost of prospecting and recruiting new members to replace retiring board members?

The best way to know what the costs are is to get a financial advisor to analyze the portfolio and show these expenses on a spreadsheet where they can be studied and understood. This is the most efficient method to quickly visualize what an enormous amount of fees are involved with the portfolio. Since these fees may not be jumping out at the CEO, who really should be concerned with them, I have compiled the following list of many of these costs.

- Cost of creating a portfolio
- Cost of people who set up the portfolio
- Cost of an investment committee, one time or continual
- Cost to monitor the portfolio
- Cost to implement changes in the mix of the portfolio
- Cost to decide the diversification of the portfolio

- Cost of the risk (standard deviation) chosen for the portfolio
- Cost of trading in the portfolio, including the obvious fees created
- Cost of turnover of equities in the portfolio (this cost is a hidden cost to the portfolio) and it is known as buy and sell cost
- Cost created by the vast number of shares in the stocks held in a mutual fund
- Cost created by the different expense ratios that are different in all of the fund classes (usually 10 classes or more)
- Cost of management fees in each fund
- Cost of 12b1 fees in many funds (they are a violation of SEC rules)
- Cost of the fund class in the portfolio, usually not known by many CEOs
- Cost of retail, index or ETF funds, (which one is owned in the portfolio?)
- Cost on different fund classes on the return
- Cost of board members
- Cost of fiduciary insurance for board members
- Cost of pension fund for board members, if offered

Do you realize the importance of the various costs discussed in the above list and paragraphs? You should now know, without a doubt, that in portfolios which are created and operated, the importance of eliminating expenses; especially when the savings are reinvested and compounded. For every dollar of cost that is reduced, the return will increase exponentially.

The cost of fiduciary coverage for not having to create a portfolio is zero. Plus, if you recall, the added bonus is that the money manager of the portfolio assumes this risk.

Now, may we explore some other costs in these organizations which affect their return? Studying the grants made by one large foundation by analyzing their 990 tax returns, I found that this foundation gave grants to over 100 other foundations. Should these grants flow through the foundation receiving the grant, thus increasing their costs? Wouldn't it be less costly if the grant went directly to the charity who will ultimately receive it? This makes me question why these organizations are trying to grow the foundation this way. I'll repeat that again. Should all philanthropic gifts go directly to the charity to reduce costs? Look at all of the operating costs in estate planning that might be put to better use. Many foundations have them.

If you already know, or are just learning the information in this book, then why would you ever donate to a foundation and not directly to a charity?

Another operation and expense that could be eliminated is fundraising. My, "think, maybe we can dodge some of this work," quote comes to mind here. If you work smart, then you don't have to work so hard, right?

What is the average cost of employees who perform fundraising? I googled this question to find out what percentage of the funds raised, on average, goes to foundation assets, and I found that number to be 67%. Therefore, we can deduce that, on average, it costs 33% to raise the funds.

The portfolio that did not have to be created, and never had a fundraiser, was able to grant an average of 8.39% from its beginning through its 20-year history. No other assets were added to the corpus.

So, can we question the size of the grants? If all grants are small, and the organization gives a lot of these grants, what is the cost of making these grants? Would this organization have to have a large number of employees to handle all of this paperwork and implementation of the grants? The page count on some large foundations' 990 tax returns exceeds 500 pages. So, that begs the question, what is the cost to pay the CPA?

If we're talking about a medium or large organization, there most likely will have to be a financial officer, thus adding more cost. This would not be true in the portfolio that doesn't have to be put together and managed.

Can we now discuss how the ready-made portfolio got started and show how so much of this cost is eliminated?

Why and how did the asset allocation strategy get its beginning? In 1990, three men won the Nobel Prize for Economics. The very next year (1991) an asset allocation was set up using the Nobel Prize total concept. The Nobel Prize was won based on the concept that you could reposition the portfolio to reduce the risk and, when this was done, the return would increase. By owning all of the classes of assets in the portfolio, they could change the percentages owned in each asset class. Now, they could change the percentage owned in each asset class to change the risk in the portfolio. By owning all of the various asset classes, it accomplished excessive diversification. By being able to control the risk, they were able to set the portfolio up in any one of these risk platforms, namely: fixed income portfolio, conservative portfolio, long term portfolio, or aggressive portfolio. This was done by changing the risk to fit these portfolios.

I recommend you look up and watch the acceptance speech and the details of the 1990 Nobel Prize online. There is an excellent paragraph in the presenter's speech while presenting the prize to these three individuals.

501(c)3

What is a 501(c)3 organization? Who can set one up (if they can qualify when completing the application)? Can they be large or small? What is the possible reason why the number of the actual 501(c)3s in the USA is very huge? Are the 501(c)3s being set up daily as this pen is writing? You bet. So, if we know the answers to some of these questions, could we have a chance to understand if there are any problems with their existence if they are not operated efficiently to satisfy why they were permitted to exist in the first place? Do I know the answers to these questions? The answer is a resounding yes! So, where am I going with this?

Rules

Being the financial advisor for an Alabama foundation, I know that it has to be a 501(c)3 organization. Are there specific rules that have to be followed to continue to operate as a 501(c)3? Yes, and the Internal Revenue Service has them file tax returns. So, if you look at the last 15 years of a foundation, beginning with the year 2007, would you be able to study how well the foundation was performing? The tax return is known as a form 990.

How many foundations in the USA are reporting assets or income? Answer is 8,577 in 2018 with $36,346,021,348 in total gross receipts. The largest foundation had $124,356,001,505.00 in assets. So, if the foundation is required to give grants of a minimum of 5% of the total assets on December 31st each year, and if we multiply the largest foundations' assets times 5%, how large is the number? You can find, research, and even print out a foundation's 990 tax return (it is public knowledge).

You should find a list of grants for that year as part of the tax return. Now, you can find out what the investment income (return on total investments) is along with how much money was obtained by fundraising. Is it important for the assets to be producing good returns, and how well are they choosing very worthy recipients to receive their grants each year?

For your information, my study of a community foundation's grants, that had close to $1 billion of assets, gave grants to over 100 other foundations that year. Can we ask, are the foundations not supposed to perform like what was proposed in the original request for approval of their 501(c)3? If we study grants in a number of foundations, can we find out how worthy that foundation is performing its duties. I have. Do you understand the importance of using the foundation very efficiently to satisfy giving permission to save taxes to set up the 501(c)3? So, are there other things about foundation performance needed to be discussed?

Long-term Operation

501(c)3s are set up for long-term operation. They can exist indefinitely as long as they operate properly. So, should the portfolio be set up so that the foundation eliminates the constant need to change the portfolio or have to set up new ones from time to time? Yes! How can this be accomplished? The foundation should find a well-diversified asset allocation portfolio, owning all of the different asset classes, with very low fund expenses. Are such funds available? Yes, and there's one with much less fund expenses than the other. What's the track record for these funds? In my opinion, it is excellent.

So, once money from a wealthy person is used to fund a 501(c)3 to possibly save estate taxes, the new organization can be operated indefinitely to accomplish the donor's wishes. The five percent (5%) distribution requirement states that it has to go to a qualified charity. This allows the donor to use the charity, or charities, of their choosing.

Cost savings in your foundation operations might possibly help you provide up to 2% of your yearly grant needs!

Why is there a need for transformation in nonprofits and foundations?

Google states the number of foundations is in the thousands and the assets held by them is in the trillions. We're not talking about a little bit of money here. 5% of one trillion is a lot of money. If costs can be eliminated in most of these foundations and nonprofits, the savings and increase in returns will be monumental!

Google states there are 28 different kinds of the 501(c)3 type of organizations. Who can even guess how many of these organizations exist? How much cost could be eliminated if just a fraction of these organizations changed their ways? Surely it could be billions. This is only part of the story!

Imagine the dollar amount of endowments that are held by various universities alone. Google quickly names three that have billions of dollars of endowment money. What I have stated so far is only the tip of the iceberg. I could go on and on. I haven't even mentioned large associations and hospitals; in fact, I found a hospital with over $8 billion in assets, and who knows if there are others out there with even more.

Let's look at the efficiency of the roughly 8,000-plus 501(c)3's total performance. First, and maybe the most important question is, are their 5% distributions going to charities that really make a difference? Are there some needs that have greater importance than the charities that are currently being funded? The answer is opinionated, but it appears to be yes.

What is the average annual investment return for the 20 years following the year 2000? Why this period? Well, this period covers several bad market corrections. What were the returns during these bad market correction times? Can this be used to require 501(c)3's to put their investment return on the 990-tax form? This would possibly eliminate using fundraising as a way to keep the 501(c)3 in existence.

If we are allowing 501(c)3s to be set up to eliminate taxes, could we expect them to produce excellent returns on all of the billions of dollars of assets that are being used? And could some of their returns be used to solve some of our national financial deficits in the USA? Is it the proper time to take another look-see? More on that in an upcoming chapter.

The growth of 501(c)3s has seemingly grown and is still growing to a point in time that analysis of their performance certainly gives the appearance of needed reform. Why not look at long term returns versus percent of fundraising cost, investment cost, financial advisor cost, software cost, hiring people to buy and sell stocks and bonds in house, lack of investigation into the recipients of the grants distributed, cost of fundraising day each year, cost of office space, equipment cost to run the foundation, salaries of management, retirement planning cost for employees, etc.?

By the way, there's another big problem looming. Are you prepared for how it will hurt fundraising?

Let's explore the impacts of the Tax Cuts and Jobs Act (TCJA) of 2017.

The most significant and noticeable change made by the TCJA was the corporate income tax rate. Under the TCJA, Congress permanently lowered the corporate tax rate from the top 35-percent to a flat 21-percent for tax years beginning after December 31, 2017.

The 2017 Tax Cuts and Jobs Act will discourage charitable giving by reducing the number of taxpayers claiming a deduction for charitable giving, and by reducing the tax savings for each dollar donated. The TCJA made major changes that discourage charitable giving relative to prior tax law.

Here are 12 reasons for concern about how the TCJA will change fundraising:

1. Far fewer wealthy people will need to give to charities to avoid estate taxes.
2. An individual's estate tax deduction is scheduled to be $11.2 million for the next 7 years, reverting back to $5.6 million in 2025.
3. The husband-and-wife estate tax deduction is scheduled to jump to $22.4 million for the next 7 years.
4. In 2000, there were 52,000 taxable estates, in 2017 there were 5,000, and it is estimated to be 1,800 in 2018. What does this trend tell us?
5. This year, when foundations seek funds, wealthy people will probably be busy changing their estate plans. Don't count on them to be as charitable as before!
6. Giving to heirs instead of charity will probably increase rapidly. Heirs will still get a step-up basis upon a donor's demise.
7. Will generation-skipping trusts and irrevocable trusts increase?
8. The new act includes tax deductions to keep up with inflation. The new act will continue allowing gifts to individuals of up to $15,000, indexed for inflation.
9. Considering all that the new act will change, will the wealthy start contributing less now to

philanthropies, like setting up Charitable Remainder Trust, Charitable Annuity Trust, and others?

10. High property and income taxes will cause some people to move to states with lower taxes. Others who are indecisive about moving may become indecisive about giving.

11. The scheduled estate tax law cut at $5.5 million in 2026 may have the ultra-wealthy nervous.

12. 2017 tax law allows individuals to give (gift) up to $11.2 million during their lifetime, before 2026.

How can foundations maintain their charitable impact when fundraising gets harder? And what if there's a market correction?

Harder fundraising as a result of the new tax act is the biggest thing to hit foundations in decades. If a market correction comes along to reduce foundation assets, the TCJA's effects will be even greater, because restoring assets through increased giving will be so much more difficult. In fact, we may be in for a correction, since the last major correction was way back in 2008. When the next correction comes, will your foundation's assets be able to take the hit? Are you sure your portfolio is totally diversified for growth while minimizing the risk of losing assets?

Another problem made worse by the new tax act is the hidden costs of buying stocks. As the wealthy cut back on giving, many foundations will finally stop ignoring how hidden stock fees sap their assets. For an excellent online article about this, see "*Hidden Expense*" by James M. Clash with Michael Malello in Forbes Magazine from January 31, 2005. Clash describes one fund with a 99% turnover and a trading cost of 32 cents per $100. He describes another with a $3.61 trading cost added to the expense ratio. When you consider the many millions of shares in a typical mutual fund, such hidden costs are astounding.

Bylaws: Are they preventing needed change?

Do your bylaws' voting rules make changing your investment strategy difficult? Then it's time to change your bylaws so your strategy can adapt to the new tax act of 2017. Commit to growth by diversifying, reducing fiduciary liability, and cutting costs. It can be done! The asset allocation strategy offers growth with minimal asset risk and will simplify decision making about turnover, stock picking, fund selection, fund removal, and conflicting investment advice from other people.

Share Classes: Does your foundation have a class that costs too much?

What share classes did mutual funds sell your foundation? Nowadays, there are more classes than A shares, B shares, and C shares — and SEC auditors are on the lookout for advisors who fail to do the best they can for their clients. If an institutional share class, which is typically associated with low fees, is better for your foundation, that is what the advisor is supposed to recommend. The right share class can help you adapt to the TCJA. The wrong share class can hurt.

A Short Story of Foundation Grants

The place to start your study is to look at the last 15 years of 990 tax returns. This is where you find a list of grants made that year and it shows the amount of the grant. Why go back 15 years? Because if you put four or five years of grants on a spreadsheet, you may find some interesting things. You may potentially find, like I did, where a community foundation many miles from another state, gave (a university) a nice grant. I know the state who received the grant for one of its universities has a big foundation. It may show a report of the same grants each year for a number of years. I've found a community foundation that has given over 100 other foundations grants for more than one year. Even though these foundations are doing these kinds of grants, they must adhere to the several IRS rules that are required for them to follow. Could we ask what amount of small grants makes sense from a cost standpoint? The spreadsheet shows some of these small grants went to one of the other 27 type 501(c)3s.

Being an advanced thinker, pressure began to mount in my still-advanced thoughts about how to share what I have learned about cost-cutting, timesaving, improved grant making, and grant effectiveness that any 501(c)3s foundation could use. So, a desire to share and teach other 501(c)3s became a burning advanced thinking process for me. After five years of effort, I ended up finding out that they did not want to use anything "new" to improve their operations. What I learned was that the portfolios were put together by good ol' boys and good ol' girls in order to pad the portfolio with large expense ratios and fee costs. Look, this has to come out of the return before they have a return!

I also learned, while trying to share my advanced thinking strategies, that they did not want any new relationships and would not entertain the idea of starting any. Just check on the Alliance of Arizona Nonprofits (501(c)3s) as to what I did to try to help them. Research the help I gave them on the state study that was done while I was in Arizona. That will speak for itself.

So, what can we do to help foundations?

If I was to sit down with a government leader or the CEO or president of a foundation board, I would ask them:

- How diversified their portfolio is, and if I may see the portfolio to confirm the diversification?
- Who established the portfolio?
- Expense-related questions relating to their operations (as previously listed in this chapter).
- Can I offer suggestions for improvement?

More often than not, my questions are intimidating to them, and the conversation stops there.

If they are willing to share, I'd first review 15 years of their tax returns, so I'd have some idea of their track record and history. Then I'd try to calculate their ROI, but that's difficult to do without first establishing what fundraising has contributed to their assets. I'd take their beginning assets and their final assets for the year and divide them to calculate their ROI, taking into account their fundraising. This will reveal the longevity of their organization, particularly if they are surviving on fundraising alone. This is usually an eye-opening revelation.

I would then educate them about the Nobel Prize winning asset allocation portfolio method. It's of utmost importance to get the Chairman of the Board educated about this new change for foundations. After many contacts and education sessions, if I am able to get the Chairman in agreement with me that "The New Prudent Man Rule" vision should be used, then the foundation is on the right path to begin benefitting from all of the aforementioned cost savings and increased returns. What a great decision and accomplishment that will be.

It's worth repeating here that the average grant for the first 20 years of using the asset allocation method was 8.39%; 3.39% greater than the 5% government requirement. **No fundraising and no**

adding to the corpus was necessary to yield pure, clean investment results.

There will certainly be end-fighting going on by some board members who don't understand "The New Prudent Man Rule" and the Nobel Prize winning asset allocation strategy; however, if the "New Advanced Thinker" (the chairman of the board) is educated on this topic, they can be very helpful and influential in regard to getting the new portfolio implemented.

My Purpose – Restated and Recapped

When I question what I have learned over the last 22 years of being a financial advisor and investment coach, my opinion is that 501(c)3s need a review and a possible overhaul. This observation is based on the performance of the foundation that I have been the advisor for these last 22 years. The 20-year average grant giving, beginning from May 2000 for the next 20 years, on their annualized return was approximately 8.39%. There is a special reason for this. The main way this foundation was organized was to eliminate cost wherever possible.

So, here is what they did:

1. Used diversified asset allocation and never had to set up a portfolio.
2. Transferred the fiduciary responsibility for managing the portfolio to the money manager of the asset allocation portfolio.
3. Did not need an investment committee.
4. Did not have to worry about diversification.
5. Did not have to remove a stock or bond nor add one back in their place.
6. It was time saving for the CEO.
7. No portfolio monitor was needed, etc.

The Bottom Line

The question becomes, what and how can an investment overview provide yearly return numbers and establish a real investment return on the vast billions of dollars now being held in the assets of 8,000-plus foundations nationwide in the USA? The answer is, if foundations would use the Nobel Prize for Economics in 1990 asset allocation and eliminate the unnecessary cost of operations, the answer to the last question is, there is no doubt what the return results would be.

Will you help me continue my quest to create, improve, and increase positive changes through the efforts of foundations and nonprofits in America?

16

A Success Story

It's about time for me to share some details as to how I have learned the information in the previous chapter. There is a little bit of a story as to how I have come to know what I have shared with you so far. It revolves around how one foundation maintained charitable giving without a single fundraiser in over 20 years.

At the age of 76, good fortune arrived in my career. I was operating my own RIA firm and an Alabama foundation handed me their assets to invest and hired me to be their advisor. The year was 2000, and you probably remember we had a large market correction that started at the beginning of that year. I had never been handed that amount of assets before. The assets were all cash, and I had to put a portfolio together because one did not exist. This is where my vision took over.

When I refer to my "vision," here is what I mean. I had already discovered the Nobel Prize information a few years prior. With my study of the concept, I decided to put my personal assets into the strategy in 1998, ultimately completing the move of all of my assets into the asset allocation fund in 1999. I already knew what costs were eliminated in the concept and how it worked. My vision kept making me think about using the Nobel Prize for the foundation's portfolio, but I knew I had a "sale" to make to be able to do this. I imagined a foundation using the asset allocation strategy and benefitting in the same way that myself and other individual investors were. I knew, without a shadow of a doubt, what cost elimination could do for a new foundation!

I knew there was some shade to be found here for this Southern insurance guy turned financial advisor. Since the foundation had no existing portfolio, this would be a great opportunity to test the Nobel Prize theory on foundations, and a chance for me to think and dodge some work associated with creating a portfolio.

When I met with the Chairman of the Board, I was thrilled to inform him that he would be transferring the Board of Director's fiduciary responsibility to the portfolio manager of the asset allocation fund. Furthermore, when I told him there was no investment committee continually needed, and no stock or bond studies were necessary, plus they wouldn't have to hire a portfolio monitor or any other administrator, I could see the wheels turning in his head. Then I drove the point home about how the asset allocation portfolio has extreme diversification; however, I think the clincher was when I told him they would have the opportunity to make a greater impact through increased giving.

Can you imagine what it was like to take such a new approach to investing? Imagine yourself as a Board member–could you really? It's one thing to try something new with your own money, but when it belongs to someone else, or another entity, that's a whole different ball game.

After several educational sessions with the Chairman of the Board, we reached an agreement to use the asset allocation for the portfolio. In arriving at the risk, I asked them to use the conservative platform (50-50) allocation.

At this same time, I was handed a large testamentary trust to advise; however, the attorneys promptly took the trust from me and set up a stock picking portfolio at a bank. Ten years later, after they learned about my ongoing success with the foundation, I was handed the same testamentary trust again. Guess what...The amount of assets in the trust was just slightly more than it was ten years before, and there were several million dollars of assets that could not be sold in order to move them. The rest is history.

Over the first six years, we went down the first two years, then up the next four years until the market was back at the point it was when it started to correct in January of 2000. By this time, we had doubled the assets in the foundation! Since that time, the few phone calls I received were not because my clients were stressing out about any downturns or questioning my decisions, rather they were calling to get large sums of cash to give for some very generous grants. May I restate, that in the first 20 years of this foundation's existence, the average annual grant percentage was 8.39% and there had not been any fundraising or additional corpus added to the account. They still had the "seed" assets they initially started with!

With that being said, let me share with you how simple it will be to get real transformation started. If you can agree to move some of your liquid assets to the asset allocation (and there are two of them to choose from), why not start and learn the concept by putting, say 25% of your assets into the allocation? It will operate just like one of the mutual funds you probably already own now.

I keep alluding to the two asset allocation funds, and, by now, you're probably wondering what they are and how you can learn more or get involved. Well, guess what, as I stated previously, they don't deal directly with the public. You have to be working with a qualified financial advisor in order to get into the game. Luckily, yours truly is here for you. Even at the age of 98, this World War II veteran is willing to help you learn how to get started cutting the unnecessary costs out of your financial operations; however, first you must realize that there is a need for transformation in your personal portfolio as well as any foundations, nonprofits, trusts or endowments you may be involved with.

Still need more proof to whet your appetite? Between the years 2000 and 2017, during that 17-year span, the aforementioned Alabama foundation has given 133% of its original investment assets to charitable organizations, and that number still continues to grow. But wait, there's more... The foundation still has 124% of its original assets remaining! And the foundation accomplished this without any fundraisers, without adding a single stock or bond to the portfolio, and without taking a one out either.

They did it by hiring me, back in 2000, to transfer their fiduciary responsibility to the Nobel Prize winning asset allocation fund. Since then, the allocation fund has managed the foundation's portfolio and provided total diversification for growth with minimal risk.

Results like these are why this particular asset allocation fund that I'm speaking of has grown to over $8.6 billion of assets under management. Their 33,000+ clients no longer gamble with their investments and financial futures. This total diversification strategy has them invested globally in 45 countries and over 16,337 holdings. Their 26-year track record of growth-with-low-risk is why its CEO is constantly sought after by investment media.

I'm slightly more accessible than the CEO of the global asset allocation fund. So, feel free to reach out to me directly if you're interested in learning more or making the best financial move of your life. You can email me at jamesrhollon@hotmail.com or call me directly at (205)-919-8661. Let's have some productive conversations about how we can work together.

Now, let's have a deeper conversation in the next chapter about how foundations and nonprofits can make a huge difference on a much larger scale.

17

Free Markets and Freedom

Having worked in foundations for over a couple of decades now, I have discovered that there are a lot of foundations in the country, and there are even more non-profits than foundations.

Most of these nonprofits are smaller operations that are run by people who are doing the same things that foundations are doing, just on a smaller scale. Many of them don't have any assets. As required by law, they must give a % of the monies they raise, much of which is done through their fundraising efforts, away to charity. In exchange, they get some pretty generous tax breaks.

When I look at how many foundations there are in the US and how many 501(c)3 nonprofits there are as well, it's mind-boggling to think about the amount of money that the government lets go tax free. My thought is, that's out of line. It's unreal. It's unfair.

My thought is, after analyzing the overall picture of these foundations and non-profit organizations, there are billions, and even trillions of dollars, of untaxed money and assets flowing through them.

Guess what... you and me, Mr. and Mrs. Taxpayer, are paying for this!

Is it fair to question if we, as a nation and as taxpayers, are getting real value out of letting people save taxes by setting up foundations? Can we compare the taxes lost in allowing 501(c)3s to be set up versus the return on the assets not taxed?

Who should accept responsibility and pay this cost? Ponder that question as I delve into a bit of history with you.

If you read the book, *Letters and Scrolls and What Archeologists Tell Us About the Bible*, you'll find in their unearthed history that there were trade routes among numerous countries and civilizations. So, we have deduced that trading has been going on since virtually the beginning of recorded history. May we then assume that there have been innovations in marketing from one generation to the next in history? I think so, yes. It seems that rulers (kings) showed favoritism and gave some freedoms to certain people under their reign. Well, where are we going with this history lesson?

Let's fast-forward to when America was being discovered and established. Was there a goal of establishing America's freedom from a foreign country? How was this done and at what cost? Was unfair taxation one of many reasons why the colonists sought independence from their old country?

Surely, we know what the cost was as America grew. History tells us that wars were waged, and many lives were lost. The colonies had to fight to establish their freedom and then continue to work at getting their "better better" during times of limited resources and hostile environments.

Skipping down through the years in which we have been free and enjoyed many benefits from our freedom, haven't there been more wars fought to keep our freedom? I'm a World War II veteran, and I fought alongside many others in order to keep freedom alive and well. So, I know a thing or two about that.

Now, can we ask what each citizen's responsibility is in regard to working to maintain freedom while enjoying the pleasures associated with being free? Should every American accept their part of the responsibility and pay their fair share of the cost of keeping America free? So, what does this have to do with marketing?

Having our freedom and being able to choose our own occupations, as well as the directions in our lives, how has this helped America become such a great country? Have you ever really thought about what happenings in our history were turning points that helped America become a great nation? If you haven't, isn't it about time to do so now?

So, how do we continue to stay free and stay great? One profound thing has happened during my lifetime of the last 98 years. What is it, you ask? I can answer your question in two words: **free markets**. Didn't the trade routes in the earliest recorded history help people and civilizations grow? Ah ha! Maybe these early examples of free markets can pave the way for how we explain what a "free market" is, how it works, and maybe even give one of the simplest examples of how it operates. I'll give it a try.

Let me start with the very simplest of examples. If I want to manufacture a pen just like the one I am writing with right now, but I do not have the assets to do so, what are my options? If it's a good pen and a worthy product, how can I acquire the funds to build the factory, purchase the machinery to build the parts, and manufacture this pen? Once the pen is made, then I must also create a marketing plan, which will require additional funds, in order to sell these pens.

Let's say my first approach is to go to some friends for help to raise money, but I am not successful. What can I do now? Well, I could sell some bonds. In that case, who gets the money? The answer is, the company. Now I owe the bondholders interest on the bond, and I must eventually return the original bond amount to the bondholder. What if I underestimate expenses and I still don't have enough money to manufacture the pen. What can I do? I can sell some stock in the company. Who gets this money? The company. What does the stockholder receive? They get a stock certificate from the company showing their fractional ownership. Where can we go with this?

Since we have free markets in America, a lot of companies have sold their stocks to the public. Who gets this money? Again, the companies get it, don't they? Well, if all the money is received by all of the companies that sold stocks in America, aren't these companies using this money to operate on? If they need more money, they sell more stock.

Now, let's look at this. A free market has been established in America for a long time now. How many companies in America have benefitted from free markets? And how many innovative products have been made as a result? Products that benefit Americans and have raised our standard of living. I believe we can truly say that free markets have been the catalyst that has made America such a great country.

Is this all of the story? No. Please read on!

We have had some great statesmen in our history. I think we can agree that some of them have come up with some very great ideas, which became laws that made it possible to do some things that have helped a lot of people. All the while, we have kept our free markets and our freedom. What an accomplishment that is.

One such brilliant idea that some wise statesman had was to establish the 501(c)3 laws. As a result, now there are 28 different types of 501(c)3s, which are helping a lot of people escape taxation on the assets held by the parties operating them. However, they are able to give 5% of their assets each year to help charities, and that is good.

There are thousands of foundations now in the US and over trillions of assets being held in them. Can you imagine the amount of money that is given to charity? What an accomplishment that is.

Look, that is only part of the story. Question – who gives more to the needy, these organizations or our US Treasury? May I add some remarks about all of this?

Since our freedom is being challenged all the time, these tax-exempt organizations who enjoy tax-free status should contribute to the preservation of the very freedom they enjoy. My thoughts are that an additional one or two percent of the income from each of these organizations should be sent to our military to help with the cost of keeping us safe and our freedom alive and well.

Here's another thought… What if foundations and nonprofits could also help curtail our outrageous national debt? As of the writing of this book, our national debt is $31.4 trillion, a tax burden of $248,000 per taxpayer, or $94,000 per citizen. Not only is it not feasible for many of us to bear this burden, but the national debt is also skyrocketing as we speak. Just visit https://www.usdebtclock.org/ and watch the numbers roll. For those of us who appreciate freedom and free markets and the greatness of the USA, this is a problem that must be solved.

If foundations and nonprofit organizations could begin to contribute to the national debt, by just one or two percent, it would make an immediate and impressive impact. After all, most taxpayers are currently contributing 28% or more of their hard-earned income, some of which is also donated to these very foundations and nonprofits. Foundations and nonprofits have benefited from tax breaks, now it's time for them to help with the national debt.

You may say, but then we'd be taking away money from grants that help charities serve those in need. Foundations and nonprofits won't be able to give as much to make our communities better.

Ah ha! If this is your thought, then maybe you haven't been paying attention to the previous chapters.

If foundations and nonprofits change their operations and cut costs and unnecessary expenses, then they will be able to continue to do the same amount of good for our charities and communities while also contributing to the good of the country as a whole. Clean up the waste and recycle it into national debt curtailment! What a grand idea, right? If used correctly, this plan eliminates waste and converts it to savings that can be applied to make a real difference.

Think, maybe we can dodge a national financial catastrophe!

If given the opportunity through ongoing freedom, our free markets will keep doing good by helping our country stay a great nation. This trend has been taking place as long as I have been alive, nearly a century now. I don't want to imagine it ever ending. But it can get much better. I have great grandkids who should be able to enjoy these same freedoms and quality of life throughout their lifetimes.

May we always keep our free markets and freedom, and may we live in better, more interesting times.

18

Dr. Van's Testimonial

My wife and I moved to Montevallo, Alabama 47 years ago. It was an opportunity for me, as a University Financial Development Officer, to be of financial assistance to a university who needed help. I will begin by stating that financial gifts from the outside to colleges and universities needed help, in general. The state deducted from the institution the amount of money raised from the outside. I had been a development officer for several universities and done development programs for them to help them raise money. I witnessed that, around these state institutions, if a gift occurred from alumni or friends, it was also deducted from the institution's budget.

At the time, James "Jim" Hollon was an insurance agent who happened to be located in Montevallo. I was introduced to him, and I immediately recognized that he was a person, rather a very professional businessman, who attracted success wherever he worked.

I recognized Jim as a person who likes to take the initiative and guide whatever program he's in.

I was charged with raising funds for the University that would stay in the private sector and be counted as funds raised by the staff. Jim had several good ideas on how we could do that at the University of Montevallo. I had started workshops on building individual foundations in each of the Universities where I had worked. The foundation gave the private sector control of the funds. At the University of Montevallo, this was readily accepted, and we were on our way to creating a foundation. Friends of the University, alumni and many others could raise funds to help.

James Hollon keenly uses his diverse skillset to accomplish his goals. Not only has he built a structure to channel funds but also to keep them under the guidance of the foundation. It was obvious that he was using his skills in the business world, and now he was transferring those skills to the foundation.

I, Dr. John VanValkenburg, had worked with foundations at previous universities and I knew that you had to have leadership skills in order to accomplish goals. At some point, we were going to turn over the guidance of the foundation that was holding the money and distribute the funds where they were needed. It was to be guided under the University foundations.

James Hollon is a person who takes ideas to the next level, and with his help, the private institutions in the state of Alabama became richer. Jim not only agreed to be a financial planner, but he would also uncover resources in the state including Boy Scouts, Fraternity organizations and others.

I could sense, right from the start, that this philosophical planner is a man of great financial interests and abilities. Jim maneuvered around neighborhoods and institutions with his creative plans. His creativeness is always shared with those in need. James Hollon became an institution of financial planning in the region, and he has positively impacted the lives of many.

19

Dear Papa,

Thank you for taking the time to inform, explain and educate me about investing.

Although I had a basic understanding of common financial terms such as stocks, mutual funds, and portfolios, the world of investing remained difficult for me to understand. I knew I needed to start saving for my future as early as possible, but I felt unsure about how to get started and how to prudently maximize my investments. That is why I am thankful that you prompted and encouraged me to study your approach to investing. I had incorrectly assumed that all investing was basically the same: either investors bought individual stocks to create their own portfolio, or they put their money in mutual funds to allow "experts" to pick stocks for them. It wasn't until you motivated me to study the investing approach you advocate that I began to realize there might be a better way.

The special projects you gave us grandchildren, the conversations around the kitchen table, and the books and online material you encouraged me to read helped convince me that passive investing through index funds in a broadly diversified portfolio allows investors to flourish financially in the long run.

I know your effort to educate others about investing is not just something you have done for your grandchildren; it is something you seek to do for your clients. I admire your desire to help and serve others through your work. This makes your work an opportunity for you to enrich the lives of your clients. This commitment to promoting investment education makes you more than an investment advisor; it makes you an investment teacher and coach.

During my research, I studied material such as Mark Heber's *Index Funds: The 12 Step Recovery Program for Active Investors*, Paul Winkler's *Above the Maddening Crowd: How to Avoid being Destroyed by the Wall Street Marketing Machine*, online educational sites such as Investopedia, and various articles and videos online. As I considered what I learned, I realized that I could narrow down the information that convinced me of the benefits of index fund investing into a few key concepts. Below, I have tried to explain these lessons in a way that those who are just beginning to consider this approach to investing might easily understand its benefits.

I hope this will serve as an educational aid for your approach to investing.

Lesson One: The Importance of Diversification and Asset Allocation

A common image of investing is that of the individual investor personally buying stock in individual companies he or she believes have good future prospects. The chances, however, of that investor finding the next superstar company and becoming wealthy by investing before a meteoric rise is quite low. A much more likely outcome is that the investor will lose money when one of the few companies in which they own stock hits hard times, or worse, goes out of business. Buying individual stocks simply exposes an investor to unneeded risks (Investopedia, "The Importance of Diversification"). This risk associated with owning stock in a few companies is unnecessary because investors can put their money in mutual funds which invest in many companies at once, perhaps even an entire segment of the market. The chances of an entire market segment imploding are much less than an individual company going under. Therefore, an investor who puts money in just a few companies has simply exposed his money to a large amount of needless risk.

While there will always be risk in investing, investors can minimize that risk through diversification, a term which refers to the process of spreading out investments across a large variety of companies or even asset classes. Investors who diversify their investments understand that some of the companies in which they invest will go under but all of the companies who succeed will help cancel out those losses. Even better than investing in a single segment of the market, the approach you use allows investors broad diversification through funds invested across many asset classes, both domestic and international. The fund that you use proudly states on their website that they have "globally diversified portfolios including over 12,000 stocks spread across more than forty countries."

Closely associated with diversification is a process known as asset allocation, a process in which a portfolio is constructed to include the mixture of asset classes appropriate to an investor's desired return and risk tolerance. Basically, asset allocation means that investors who choose a portfolio with a higher percentage of equities (e.g. stocks) take on a higher degree of risk but hope to be rewarded with great returns in the long run. Typically, younger investors who can afford for their savings to fall during downturns in the market (and thus have a higher risk tolerance) choose an asset allocation with a high percentage of stocks. Investors nearing retirement tend to be more risk averse (lower risk tolerance) and more interested in conserving rather than growing their wealth. These investors typically choose an asset allocation with a lower percentage of stocks but a higher the percentage of fixed income investments (ex: bonds) which promise less reward but are also less risky.

When done well, asset allocation provides investors with the greatest amount of return for the lowest amount of risk. The economic theory behind this concept is called the Modern Portfolio Theory. This theory, for which Harry Markowitz, Merton Miller and William Sharpe won the Nobel Prize in 1990, asserts that proper diversification can maximize returns for given levels of risk along what came to be known as the "Efficient Frontier". In other words, diversification and asset allocation are supremely important because diversification can reduce the risk of a portfolio without reducing the expected return.

In summary, broad diversification and appropriate asset allocation shield investors from unnecessary risk and enable them to maximize returns.

Lesson Two: It is Very Difficult to Outperform the Market but Quite Possible to Mirror It.

Many investors believe the trick to investing is to outperform the market by buying stocks before they go up in price and selling before they go down. They attempt to analyze the news and company performance in order to buy undervalued and sell overvalued stock. This type of investing is called "active" investing. If individual investors are not confident that they can select the right stocks or market segments themselves, they invest in mutual funds in order to allow experts (the mutual fund managers) to do it for them. One of the most startling discoveries I made in my research was the idea that it is extremely difficult, even for financial experts, for such active investing to outperform the average return of the market in the long run. Moreover, it is very easy, and in fact quite common, for actively managed funds to underperform the market. Investopedia's article, "*Index Investing: Index*

Funds" asserts, "The truth is that a majority of mutual funds fail to outperform the S&P 500. The exact stats vary depending on the year, but on average, anywhere from 50%-80% of funds get beat by the market." That is a significant amount of funds underperforming the market average. Coming to terms with the idea that active investing routinely fails to deliver on its promise to outperform the market dramatically changed my view of investing.

Why is it so difficult for active managers to beat the market averages? Eugene Fama proposed a theory known as the Efficient Market Hypothesis to explain this. This hypothesis asserts that a fair and free market is very good at setting stock prices because all of the available information which affects the stock price is quickly and efficiently incorporated into that price. If true, then investors should assume that at any given moment all stock prices accurately reflect the true value of that stock. This makes finding undervalued stocks or undervalued market segments very difficult. An article in Investopedia states the case this way: "Attempts to systematically identify and exploit stocks that are mispriced on the basis of information typically fail because stock price movements are largely random and are primarily driven by unforeseen events" (Investopedia, "Passive Management").

If stock prices are indeed driven by "unforeseen events" (e.g. no one can know them ahead of time), and if the information from these events is almost immediately reflected in each stock's price, then it follows that it would be difficult to know for sure if the price of a stock or market segment is about to go up or down. If true, the Efficient Market Hypothesis undercuts the philosophy and promise behind active investing.

In contrast to active investing, fund managers may choose to simply attempt to mirror the market such that they get the average return of the market. Since these managers do not hunt for the next deal or try to guess what's on the horizon in order to sell before a market downturn, simply tracking the returns of a certain market segment instead, this approach is called passive investing. Funds created to mirror a certain market segment (market index) are called index funds. Since these funds follow a certain index, if that market segment goes up, the index fund goes up in the same amount. If that market segment goes down, the fund goes down. All the index fund manager needs to do is to make sure the index fund follows the market segment it is seeking to mirror. Simply earning market averages may not sound flashy, but it is startling to think that those investors who did would come out better over the long haul than most active investors.

Another common, negative side-effect of active investing through mutual funds is a concept known as "style drift." Understandably, managers engaged in active investing work under constant pressure to have their funds outperform the market. If they consistently underperform the market, they will likely run out of customers who are willing to invest in their funds. Therefore, active managers may succumb to the temptation to invest in whatever they consider to be the current "hot" segment of the market, regardless of the stated purpose of the fund and expectations of its investors. For example, an investor may wish to invest in a mutual fund consisting mainly of large US companies; however, if that segment of the market begins to decline and another segment of the market begins to take off, the manager may begin to change the make-up of the fund by investing more heavily in that rising segment (say international companies). If this process continues, the investors become increasingly invested in segments of the market they hadn't signed up for and may feel are too risky or too conservative. A fund that falls into this pattern is said to have "drifted" from its original make-up. A passively managed index fund, however, simply follows its segment of the market whether it goes up or down. The passive manager is under no pressure to beat the market, thus decreasing the danger of style drift.

Lesson Three: Invest Based on Academic Research, Not Managerial Skill.

The actively managed investing industry competes for customers, and thus, actively managed funds may seek to acquire new customers through marketing campaigns or favorable media coverage (Paul Winkler, *Above the Maddening Crowd: How to Avoid being Destroyed by the Wall Street Marketing Machine*, chapter 4). Proponents of active investing point to funds or fund managers that have a track record of high returns. The emphasis is on fund performance and managerial skill at stock picking and market timing. On the other hand, advocates of passive investing through index funds make their appeal based on academic research. In fact, one of the most interesting aspects of my research has been realizing the breadth and depth of the academic research that supports a passive investment approach using index funds in a broadly diversified portfolio. For example, one fund adheres to an investment philosophy it calls The Free Market Portfolio Theory. The Free Market Portfolio Theory is the synthesis of three academic principles: Efficient Market Hypothesis, Modern Portfolio Theory, and the Three-Factor Model. Together these concepts form a powerful, disciplined and diversified approach to investing. Notice the appeal is not based on extolling the superior talents of its managers but rather on the economic research of Eugene Fama (Efficient Market Hypothesis), Harry Markowitz, Merton Miller and William Sharpe (Modern Portfolio Theory) and Eugene Fama and Kenneth French (Three-Factor Model).

Understanding these theories gives me confidence in the passive approach to investing through index funds because it is based primarily on academic theory rather than the skill of any one manager or staff.

Lesson Four: Expenses Can Eat up Your Earnings

I was quite surprised to read that, in 2014, Warren Buffett praised passive investing through index funds. In a letter to his shareholders, Buffet gave the following instructions about how he would like his estate managed after his death: "My advice to the trustee couldn't be more simple: Put 10% of the cash in short-term government bonds and 90% in a very low-cost S&P 500 index fund. [...] I believe the trust's long-term results from this policy will be superior to those attained by most investors [...] who employ high-fee managers" (from an article on m@rketwatch.com titled "*Warren Buffett to heirs: Put my estate in index funds*"). Not only is it amazing that one of the most famous active investors praised index funds, but this quote brings up another important benefit of passive investing, namely lower expenses.

As a rule, actively managed funds will have higher expenses than passively managed funds. Two common examples of such expenses are management fees and transaction costs. (Investopedia, "*Index Investing: Index Funds*" and "*Portfolio Turnover*"). As Buffett points out, mutual funds can be run by "high-fee managers."

Management fees are what fund managers charge investors for managing their money. Active managers require more compensation for all of the time spent researching stocks and market trends in order to try and outperform the market. If active managers had a great track record at being able to provide their clients with returns significantly above the market average, these management fees would be justified. However, given what has already been said above regarding the ability of active investing to outperform the market, it does not seem prudent to pay this higher fee. Passive managers charge less fees because they know exactly what to invest in. There is no guesswork needed to try and outperform the market. The passive managers simply need to construct and maintain a fund which mirrors the returns of a particular index.

In addition to management fees, actively managed mutual funds may incur significant transaction costs. These are costs that occur each time a stock is sold. Passively managed funds tend to incur fewer transaction costs than actively managed funds because passive managers basically maintain the stocks in their funds while active managers might buy and sell stocks more frequently in order to try and beat the market.

In Closing:

Papa, I admire and appreciate the fact that you are a life-long learner and continue to encourage your family to be life-long learners. You have a keen sense of curiosity about the world, and I am thankful that you seek to develop that sense of curiosity and commitment to continual self-education in your family. The projects you asked us to do, the questions you ask to stimulate our thinking, and the resources you have pointed us to have grown my curiosity about investing. What had seemed overwhelming and intimidating now feels interesting and important. I am grateful and excited to be able to explain investment concepts to my family, friends and colleagues. Thank you for being an investment teacher and coach. I know that your efforts have not only benefited your grandchildren but will also benefit the next generation as I plan to pass on what I have learned to my children.

Much love, your grandson, Charlton

Acknowledgements

So many people have been influential and supportive in my life; the list is long and filled with advanced thinkers, stalwart leaders, generous donors, action takers, and inspirational people. There are simply too many people for me to even attempt to thank them all; however, the following people were instrumental in the creation of this book.

My deceased first wife, Betty Espy Hollon, gave me a priceless gift of three wonderful sons. I cherish the years we spent together as a family. You are still an inspiration to me, and you will always hold a special place in my heart.

I owe my son, James H. Hollon, a big thank you for the title of this book. He was the first one to walk in my kitchen and question the fruits of my labor when he noticed that I had cooked some home-grown yellow squash and thrown raisins into the mix. This experimental recipe turned out to be quite delicious and the phrase "raisins in the squash" has become an analogy for my unique strategies and willingness to take chances and try new things. It's also a cherished family quote that always invokes a bit of laughter!

My three sons, James, Tom, and Kim, along with my grandchildren and great grandchildren are the objects of my affection. They inspire me daily to continue my quest to better this world for our future generations. These three men, their children, and their children's children are more than capable of continuing my legacy. In particular, I want to thank my grandson, Charlton, for urging me to write another book and incorporate some of my life experiences and stories. His two contributions bookend this work brilliantly.

I want to convey a priceless appreciation for my wife, Shirley, who, with a great deal of patience, has helped me tremendously in every facet, particularly in the technology realm. Whether it's receiving or sending emails, researching data online, or running errands to Office Depot for printing and supplies, she is there for me. This book would not have been possible without her.

Shirley's son, Wayne Jones, is my stepson, and he has been a wonderful addition to my family. Thank you for your support.

Roy McBryar is my attorney and the RIA of my business. His legal advice and counseling have always been a key element in ensuring that my clients, their assets, and myself and my own assets are protected and in compliance with legal requirements.

Dr. Gordon Klingenschmitt "Dr. Chaps" has been a wonderful friend and colleague over the years. Thank you for always being there for me, and I greatly appreciate you writing the foreword for this book.

Dr. John VanValkenburg gave me the opportunity to help and participate in some university initiatives. Thank you for your trust and the wonderful collaboration.

Billy Lambert is the chairman of the board of the foundation that I represent. He has been my confidant all the way. His trust in me and his willingness to entertain and adopt my out-of-the-box strategies is testament to this man's desire to stay on the cutting edge of foundation growth. Through his generosity and grants, much good has been done for others.

Thank you to all of my clients who have hired me and entrusted me with the privilege of managing and growing their assets. It is truly an honor to work with you.

I'd also like to thank my friend and colleague, Andy Andrews, who is an internationally known speaker and bestselling author, for working with me in the past, and for recently connecting me with my ghostwriter, Sean Donovan.

Speaking of Sean Donovan, I'd like to give him a lot of credit for crystallizing my thoughts, ideas, stories, and notes into the words on the pages of this book. Communication between us during the ghostwriting process flowed like the mighty Mississippi, with ease and fluidity. It has been a pleasure and genuine joy working together with him. Additionally, I'd like to thank his wife, Thays Franca, for her artistic input and graphic design of the book cover.

I'd be remiss if I didn't thank you, dear reader, for investing your time and attention to the pages of this book. Without you, this effort is meaningless. I hope you are now empowered to take control of your financial future. My hope is that you will also be inspired to do some good in the world with your future success. Together, we can create a legacy that will ensure a better world for our future generations.

My Declaration

I, James R. Hollon, declare the possibility of being able to share an example of a foundation using Nobel Prize winning principles for almost two decades.

I stand for promoting better diversification of charitable assets to have a breakthrough in <u>much improved returns at less cost and risk.</u>

I can be counted on to continue sharing this winning example as long as my health will permit.

I am committed to never quit trying to do everything I can for charity. May I share this example with you?

Contact:
Jamesrhollon@hotmail.com
(205)-492-7916
(205)-919-8661

Made in United States
Orlando, FL
28 December 2022

27659867R00124